By the same author

POLITICAL PRESSURE AND ECONOMIC POLICY:
British Government, 1970–74

*THE LABOUR GOVERNMENT, 1974–79:
Political Aims and Economic Reality

THE FIRST THATCHER GOVERNMENT, 1979–83:
Contemporary Conservatism and Economic Change

Also published by Macmillan

THATCHERISM

Scope and Limits, 1983–87

Martin Holmes

Senior Visiting Research Fellow
Mansfield College, Oxford

First published 1989

Published by
THE MACMILLAN PRESS LTD
Houndmills, Basingstoke, Hampshire RG21 2XS
and London
Companies and representatives
throughout the world

Typeset by Footnote Graphics,
Warminster, Wilts

Printed in the People's Republic of China

British Library Cataloguing in Publication Data
Holmes, Martin, *1954–*
Thatcherism: scope and limits, 1983–1987.
1. Great Britain. Economic policies,
1983–1987
I. Title
330.941'0858
ISBN 0–333–49232–3 (hardcover)
ISBN 0–333–49233–1 (paperback)

CONTENTS

ACKNOWLEDGEMENTS

Many people have greatly assisted me in the writing of this book, not least the many Cabinet ministers, junior ministers, backbench MPs, civil servants and Conservative Party officials who gave their time to be interviewed.

I am particularly indebted, however, to Fennella Morris who was a most diligent research assistant, to Jane Varley who read and commented constructively on an earlier draft, and to my trio of superb secretarial assistants, Jackie Brentnall, Sarah Cramer and Sally Barker. Marie Schulte prepared the index with speed and precision.

I would also like to thank the Principal and Fellows of Mansfield College for providing an atmosphere conducive to scholarship and appreciative of research. Tim Farmiloe at the publishers handled the manuscript with customary courtesy and efficiency and I am grateful to him.

Needless to say any errors in the following pages are my responsibility alone.

Martin Holmes
Mansfield College
Oxford

INTRODUCTION

By the time Mrs Thatcher had won her third consecutive election victory in June 1987, she had been Prime Minister eight years, party leader twelve years, and had given her name to an unmistakable political phenomenon – Thatcherism. So much has already been written about the origins, nature and aims of Thatcherism that yet another book about it requires justification. For this author, however, Thatcherism is, and always has been, more than the political career and philosophical statements of Margaret Thatcher. It has embodied the transformation of Britain's post-war centre-left consensus into the Thatcherite dream of a property-owning, meritocratic, entrepreneurial, market-oriented society.

This development has already been chronicled in this author's three previous books. In the first, a study of the Heath Government,[1] the crisis in the Conservative Party as it moved swiftly leftwards under Heath after the 1971 U-turns, was analysed in the context of a party defeated four times out of five General Elections, but still retaining its belief that it was Britain's natural party of government. The events of 1970–4 led directly to the overthrow of the Heath leadership by Mrs Thatcher in 1975 and contain the seeds of Thatcherism.

The second book,[2] traced the agonised, but temporary, retreat away from Keynesian economics by the 1974–9 Labour Government, culminating in the 1976 IMF crisis which proved an intellectual dry run for Thatcherite economic thought. Yet the political agenda of 1974–9 was still essentially corporatist, with the great power of the trade union movement ultimately proportional to its own unpopularity in the 1978–9 Winter of Discontent. The 1979 General Election proved that Thatcherism was not unelectable, as the Conservative left had long argued.

The third book[3] studied the first Thatcher Government in the dual context of the evolution of Conservative philosophy and the economic changes inherent in Thatcherite policy in terms of the deliberate break-up of the post-war consensus on full employment, trade-union power, and industrial interventionism. In each of the three books, attention was paid to the economic policy machine and the ultimate relationship between economic policy and the electoral prospects for the party in office. And to be sure, these aspects are also present in this book.

However, as Thatcherism has developed from a rebellion against Heath to a governmental creed, and finally to a political phenomenon, so many of its mysteries have been clarified. Thatcherism is now de-mystified, little of it uncharted politically or unexplainable. This study therefore aims to analyse Thatcherism in the 1983–7 period only in terms of why specific policies were adopted or why more obvious areas of reform were neglected. As such, this is not a general book; its does not aim at a Cook's tour overview of Thatcherism. The intention is to assess the scope of Thatcherism in a number of key policy areas but also to explore what sort of limits have prevented Thatcherism from either totally transforming British society or from radically altering the political system itself.

More so than 'Butskellism', or even 'democratic socialism', Thatcherism excites political controversy by wilfully challenging accepted centre-left establishment thinking. Any book on Thatcherism, therefore, is unlikely to be totally aloof from the policy changes it describes. This book has not attempted any contrived neutralism and while that lays it open to criticism of a certain sort, it also hopes to demonstrate that academic analysis does not lack rigour as soon as controversial topics are tackled. Thatcherism is too important to be left only to those who see it in a vacuum of impersonal political impulses from which lessons can never be drawn. Fully to understand Thatcherism, including its scope and limits, is to realise that the political passions it arouses are a part of, not separate from, its reality.

PART I

The Scope of Thatcherism

CHAPTER 1

Thatcherism Defined

A volume of literature already exists on the nature of Thatcherism and lack of definition has never been a characteristic that has inhibited analysis. Peter Riddell sees Thatcherism as 'an instinct, a series of moral values and ... an expression of Mrs. Thatcher's upbringing in Grantham, her background of hard work and family responsibility, ambition and postponed satisfaction, duty and patriotism'.[1] Riddell's Thatcherism is a conglomeration of feelings and prejudices rather than a coherent, viable ideology. Undoubtedly there are elements of instinct and gut feeling in Mrs Thatcher's personal approach to politics, and these have indeed contributed to the totality of Thatcherism. Similarly, Peter Jenkins, also a generally unsympathetic critic of Thatcherism, regards it as 'more a style than an ideology'. For Jenkins, Thatcherism is based on a conspiracy theory which blamed Britain's decline on a multitude of bogeys from trade-union power and inflationary economic polices to permissiveness and declining family standards. Suburban prejudice rather than any definable ideology has nevertheless been successful in 'the end of the Socialist era'.[2]

But as an ideology, Thatcherism has taken clearer shape than a mere collection of middle-class convictions. Dennis Kavanagh has discerned that 'few doubt that Mrs. Thatcher has a coherent set of political ideas and that these guide her behaviour'.[3] He isolates eight elements of her belief system, based on minimal government, the importance of individual responsibility, a strong state to provide adequate defence and to uphold the rule of law, the promotion of a market economy, the moral rejection of high borrowing, and the pursuit of lower taxes and sound money. Kavanagh also argues, with much justification, that Thatcherism is a negative reaction to aspects of the post-war consensus such as Keynesian economics, excessive welfare spending and trade-union abuses of power. Thatcherism he sees as a reaction to perceived failures of public policy after 1945.

3

Similarly, Robert Skidelsky prefers to see Thatcherism as the culmination of a period of 'gestation' and, as such, portrays it as a reaction to previous crises and events. He argues that:

As we know, the Thatcher age has ushered in the sharpest break with consensus politics since the war. This is not to say that everything the Thatcher government has done would not have been done by some other government. Some change of direction was inevitable in the face of accelerating inflation; the accumulating crisis in the economy, in industrial relations, and in government and local authority finances; and of longer-term socio-economic changes.

'Monetarism' started under Callaghan, as did the first resolute attempt to rein in public spending. (It was Anthony Crosland who told the local authorities that 'the party is over'.) Trade union reform was on the agenda long before Mrs. Thatcher implemented it. The collapse of Callaghan's pay policy in the 'winter of discontent' made it unlikely that any successor government would return in a hurry to incomes policy. In social policy, the sale of council houses to tenants was seriously considered by both Wilson and Callaghan; it was Callaghan who started the debate on the 'quality' of education.

So the Thatcher Revolution had been gestating in previous governments and in previous events. Nevertheless, the Thatcher approach to government was distinguished by a quite different ideological temper. It was based on a rejection of corporatism, a much greater reliance on market forces, a robust assertion of the values of self-help and self-reliance, and an appeal to the idea of 'strong but limited' government. [4]

For John Cole, the repudiation of the Heath years is central to understanding Thatcherism. The removal of Heath, Cole argues, was not just personal but represented an intellectual reaction to the economic policies pursued by Conservative governments since 1945. Consequently, Mrs Thatcher came to power 'in the grip of a theory . . . [an] economic and political revolution leading to a revival of Britain and the final defeat of Socialism that Mrs. Thatcher had set her heart [on]'. [5]

This view is disputed by some writers. Julius Gould and Digby Anderson, while sympathetic to what is known as Thatcherism, prefer to maintain that Mrs Thatcher's shifting and inconsistent assumptions do not amount to an 'ism' or ideology. They see instead a mixture of ideas which suggest a dichotomy between Thatcherism that is and a Thatcherism that might have been.[6] Gould and Anderson see the achievements of Thatcherism as limited. The failure to challenge the monopolistic price setting of labour, the inability to radicalise the welfare state, the neglect of properly culling the quangos, and the retreat from educational vouchers demonstrate that Mrs Thatcher did not really possess a 'full blown doctrine'.[7] Kenneth Minogue goes as far as to argue that 'it is not the least of the paradoxes of her period of rule that the project of diminishing government has often led to an actual increase in the range of governmental intervention'.[8]

However, it may be pointed out, according to Samuel Finer, that Thatcherism does mark a radical departure of an ideological kind because of the contrast with the Keynesian era which preceded 1979. 'In brief', Finer argues, 'Thatcherism introduced a wholly new economic theory and practice and pursued them with obduracy and consistency'.[9] For Finer the practice of Thatcherism makes it a radical ideology, whereas for Gould and Anderson the lack of a predetermined philosophy is not compensated for by specific reforms in government.

A synthesis of these views is provided by David Howell who considers that Thatcherism was ideologically determined to break the post-war consensus but then, in government, became sidetracked by technicalities such as different ways of measuring the money supply and an over emphasis on PSBR reduction. Howell castigates Thatcherism in office for becoming obsessed with method not substance. Particularly, the concern with macroeconomic aggregators – in themselves notoriously difficult to ascertain – has diverted the radicalism of 1979 into what Howell calls a 'blind victory'.[10]

British Conservatives have long debated the nature of 'true Conservatism' and the desirability of ideological or pragmatic approaches to governing. Partly because Thatcherism is perceived as ideological, the current debate within the party has often been acrimonious. Jim Prior has written that his 'overriding desire has been to work with the grain of society, to plane down the causes of conflict and to create amongst people a sense that they matter and that their wishes are being taken into account by government'.[11]

For Prior, the conflict and confrontational nature of the Thatcher years has been both a personal and political anathema. With greater bitterness, Francis Pym has castigated Thatcherism as a 'narrow and dogmatic faction' and Mrs Thatcher as 'an absolutist [who] likes everything to be clear cut: absolutely in favour of one thing, absolutely against another. It is the opposite of my approach'.[12] Much of Pym's book amounted to an attack on free-market economics, balanced, so as to appeal to a Conservative readership, by obligatory critical references to Marxist ideology. Michael Heseltine, also, has strongly attacked Mrs Thatcher's economic policy, though the cause of his resignation during the 1986 Westland crisis was the manner of Mrs Thatcher's Prime Ministerial autocracy.

However, the internal ideological battle over the desirability or otherwise of Thatcherism has moved on. The 'dries versus wets' battle of the first Thatcher administration, which concerned such matters as monetary policy, has now broadened to encompass more general and philosophical aspects. The wets stress a paternalistic, One Nation, Toryism with the emphasis on a stable and harmonious society. The Thatcherites now stress a different state of nature, based on fundamental tenets as a guide to action. Mrs Thatcher herself has described Thatcherism in this way. In an interview with Rodney Tyler, she expressed the conviction that:

We've been working to restore the political system to bring out all that was best in the British character. That's what we've done. It's called Thatcherism – it's got nothing to do with Thatcher except that I was merely the vehicle for it. But it is in everything I do. It's a mixture of fundamentally sound economics. You live within your means; you have honest money, so therefore you don't make reckless promises. You recognise human nature is such that it needs incentives to work harder, so you cut your tax. It is about being worthwhile and honourable. And about the family. And about that something which is really rather unique and enterprising in the British character – it's about how we built an Empire, and how we gave sound administration and sound law to large areas of the world. All those things are still there in the British people aren't they?[13]

The more general and wide-ranging definitions of Thatcherism have been particularly seized on by Marxist, or far left Socialist, critics. Such writers see Thatcherism as establishing an illiberal strong state, waging class warfare against the working class and progressive groups such as feminists, homosexuals and ethnic minorities. Thatcherism is regarded as a form of social control of which market disciplines are only one exposition. Tony Benn, for example, has described Thatcherism in the context of the patriotism surrounding the Falklands War, as pure fascism. Arthur Scargill, speaking at the start of the 1984–5 miners' strike, advocated that:

> To defeat them [the Tories] it will take people and cash on a mammoth scale. Every sinew in every factory, office, dole queue, docks, railway, plant and mill will need to be strained to the maximum. Waiting in the wings are four million unemployed whose numbers could swell the picket lines at any time ... What is urgently needed is the rapid and total mobilisation of the trade union and Labour movement to take positive advantage of the unique opportunity to defend our class and roll back the machinery of oppression, exploitation and deep-seated human misery.[14]

The view of Thatcherism as an engine of repression is argued by Marxists such as Levitas, Hall and Jacques, and Gamble.[15] To such writers, the social authoritarianism of Thatcherism is mobilised by a variety of weapons, including the waging of an economic war against the working class by the creation of high unemployment and the resort to market discipline. Martin Jacques, the editor of *Marxism Today*, sees Thatcherism as self-regenerating ideology, planned in advance to achieve its class aims:

> Its first term was about extolling sacrifice, lowering expectations, and promoting the market. The second was about privatisation (which hardly figured in the first term), the new divisions, and the emergence of a prosperous majority with a seemingly voracious consumer appetite. The third will be about that still unconquered stronghold of social democracy, the welfare state.
>   Herein lies one of the great strengths of Thatcherism, a sign of its political endurance and durability, its capacity not only to

think strategically but to renew itself long after the point where previous governments had lost any sense of political direction or energy.[16]

Jacques's argument, though unsophisticated, does contain germs of truth. *Ad hoc* or circumstantial explanations of political phenomena have never been, after all, a feature of Marxist analysis.

To many writers on the left, Thatcherism is profoundly undemocratic and, given the opportunity, would welcome a strong state on the Chilean model of military dictator, General Pinochet. Although the evidence for such claims is dubious, not least because of Mrs Thatcher's populism and her successive election victories according to accepted electoral law, the Marxist view of Thatcherism as social authoritarianism has achieved a wider political currency because of Mrs Thatcher's allegedly 'uncaring' image and her forceful and robust style of highly personalised leadership. In parliamentary terms, the most consistent exponent of this view has been the Labour backbencher Tam Dalyell, who has utilised his freedom to attack Mrs Thatcher's 'sinister pattern of deceit'[17] in a way that Labour frontbenchers cannot, because of the rules governing unparliamentary behaviour.

It is clear, therefore, that while a degree of consensus exists on the general nature of Thatcherism, there is still a high level of disagreement as to its exact nature. Is it an ideology or not? Is it a new departure from the Butskellite consensus or the culmination of a gestation period foreshadowing change? Is it primarily economic or rather more social, with stress on the family and codes of societal behaviour? Is it a liberating individualism rolling back an oppressive socialist state, or is it a form of fascism, or semi-fascism, aiming at repression?

Such questions are not easy to answer, as the many books on Thatcherism (including this one) demonstrate. For this author, Thatcherism *is* a full-blown ideology which *does* depart radically from the post-war consensus in a way that Mr Heath's Selsdon man (1970–1), or Mr Callaghan's monetarist experiment (1976–8) did not. Thatcherism is both reactive to the failures of Keynesian political economy, including those of Conservative administrations, but also visionary, in aiming at a different economy and society. However, Thatcherism is not the simple aggregation of Mrs Thatcher's policy speeches and individual preferences – for capital punishment in a free vote, for example. It is as facile to argue that Thatcherism is what Mrs Thatcher does as to argue that socialism is what a Labour government does. Thatcherism is not a total package either to be accepted in whole or rejected outright. Mrs Thatcher, for example, has supported the restoration of capital punishment and favoured curbs on the televised broadcasting of sexually explicit or violent programmes. Some Thatcherites may agree with such policies but others, equally, may not. Similarly, some Thatcherites favour tougher immigration restrictions to prevent added racial tension, while others, for free-market economic reasons, favour increased immigration of entrepreneurial ethnic groups – Chinese, Vietnamese, and so on. Some Thatcherites prefer to maintain the existing prohibition on building on Green Belt land while concentrating development in the inner cities; others see the removal of planning controls as central to the rolling back of the Socialist state. Thatcherism is not a total package with a pre-ordained policy prescription for every topical controversy. Instead it is a specific ideology of a few central tenets.

The essence of Thatcherism is the advocacy of a market economy, where the state fulfills strictly limited functions such as monetary control, the upholding of the rule of law, and the provision of the defence of the realm. From this basic definition, two main consequences are observable. Firstly, in the context of Britain 1945–79, Thatcherism was inevitably bound to be ideological. As an intellectual descendant of Adam Smith's free market-vision, Thatcherism could not help but challenge the postwar consensus based on nationalisation, Keynesian economics, government regulation and planning, the provision of universal, rather than needs-based, selected welfare. Thatcherism can thus be seen as an ideological rejection of socialism in its first stage and as the engine for free-market economics once the Socialist state had been rolled back by a Thatcher administration. As Alan Walters has pointed out, such an ambitious programme is long term. He notes that 'the policy of the Conservative government envisaged a long period, perhaps as long as eight or ten years, in which major reforms would be completed. Mrs Thatcher's government of 1979–83 was only the start of this long programme of reform'.[18] Secondly, Thatcherism has had to be populist in order to maintain power in an electoral system suited to the competitive bidding process by politicians promising ever more to specific groups of the electorate by way of the redistribution of wealth. The basic ideology of Thatcherism had to promote free enterprise not just as an intellectual abstraction from the 19th century, but as electorally appealing in an age of mass democracy and rising social and economic expectations. As will be discussed in Chapter 8, this process has raised the Conservative vote from the 36 per cent (and declining) of Mr Heath's leadership, to a steady, winning, though short of majoritarian, percentage. In fact, the stability of the Conservative vote indicates that the popularity of Thatcherism has a strong, but currently not expanding, appeal. In 1979, the Conservative vote stood at 44 per cent, in 1983, 42 per cent, and in 1987, 43 per cent. Although by-election and opinion poll evidence between general elections suggests electoral volatility, those general election figures certainly disprove the view of Thatcherism as universally hated or capable of only a temporary electoral success. Dennis Kavanagh, although no Thatcherite himself, has cogently argued that:

> There is some evidence that Mrs. Thatcher has attracted a particular electoral constituency. That section of the middle class which includes shopkeepers, foremen, and the small self-employed businessmen – the petit bourgeois – has turned strongly to the party since she became leader. In 1974 such people had been disillusioned with the Heath government. A survey study of the 1983 election found that this section was the most right-wing of all on questions about privatisation, incentives versus equality, trade unions, and comprehensive schools, and over 70% voted Conservative in 1983. There have been other gainers; holders of shares, homeowners, and those in work, whose real take-home pay increased by 5% on average over the life of the 1979 government.[19]

It should also be realised that with one in ten of the workforce numbering 2.6 million now self-employed and with the decline in manual jobs, particularly in the nationalised industries, the socio-economic trends in the long term may favour an increase in the Conservative vote. While recent evidence suggests that the Conservative vote is roughly static, an increase is as likely as a decrease in the next decade.

Both the two main strands of Thatcherism which flow from its basic definition – its combative ideological nature and its need to be populist – have clearly been reflected in Mrs Thatcher's leadership style. Not surprisingly, Mrs Thatcher exudes the crusading aspect of Thatcherite ideology, and is not afraid of repetition of aphorisms and simple injunctions – hard work, the limits of government spending, the importance of sound money. These epithets have been dubbed 'corner shop economics' by her opponents (in all parties), while her supporters accept that any attack on socialism has had to face head on the need to explain both the limits of government and the extent of individual entrepreneurial responsibility. Thatcherism has therefore fought socialism at two levels. Intellectually it has shifted the argument away from the inevitability of a collectivist society on to the failures of socialist and Keynesian nostrums. The New Right intellectualism is a manifestation of this trend. But Thatcherism has also had to persuade the overwhelming mass of apolitical citizens that they will be better off under Thatcherism, and better governed. The sale of council houses and the popularity of privatisation share floatations are manifestations of this development.

Mrs Thatcher's leadership style has provided notions of strong leadership purposefully directed towards particular economic goals ideologically different from those pursued before 1979. If this style is regarded as hectoring, crude, repetitive and uncaring it is a backhanded tribute to its success in challenging a consensus politics which sought to explain away conflict and to compromise on fundamental issues. Thus both Arthur Scargill and Mrs Thatcher shared in common an ideological belief system which rejected the corporatist consensus. Although their ideologies were diametrically opposed, the necessity of sticking to them was unquestionable. It is this ideological aspect of Thatcherism (and Scargillism) that makes so many in the centre of British politics uneasy. The idea of an industrial victory, rather than a compromise, is alien to consensus politics. Thatcherism expressly rejects the view that men of goodwill sitting round a table can, by reasonableness and compromise, solve economic and industrial problems. Conversely, many on the Labour left admire Thatcherism for 'fighting for its class', something that previous Labour governments should have done for the 'working class'.

As far as the left's main objection to Thatcherism is concerned

– the development of an authoritarian and repressive state – any judgement depends on one's own political sympathies. The question of liberties and freedoms has always produced conflicting definitions in British politics. Is it the liberty of the woman to have an abortion, or the right of the unborn child to live? Is it the right to picket forcefully and effectively or the right of workers to work in defiance of their union? Is it the right of *habeas corpus* or the necessity of the Prevention of Terrorism Act? Is it the right of the National Front to march through immigrant areas or the right of the residents to pursue their daily lives unmolested and without menace? These and other questions show that rights and liberties conflict according to definition. The Thatcherite experience reflects this. Picketing and the use of the police to protect working miners have conflicted. The GCHQ union rights have clashed with the paramount duty to maximise effective defence and intelligence gathering. Moreover, Thatcherites can claim that the introduction of secret ballots before strikes has increased the level of democracy and that the former permanent tenantry in council houses has been liberated from petty and stifling restrictions by the right to buy.

Although the debate on rights and liberties is almost unamenable to common definitions in the British context, it may be pointed out that the left's attack on the Thatcherite 'strong state' could also be made on the consensus governments of the post-1945 era. As Peter Hain points out, the Attlee Governments used troops to break the 1949 dock strike.[20] The Callaghan Government sought to prevent entry to Britain of Hosenball and Agee in the name of national security. Mr Heath's corporatist Government imprisoned the 'Pentonville Five' and invoked five states of emergency in three and a half years. Mrs Thatcher has studiously avoided imprisoning individual trade unionists and has yet to use emergency powers. The Wilson and Callaghan Governments failed, despite manifesto promises, to reform the Official Secrets Act. In 1977, Jim Callaghan used troops to break the firemen's strike, despite the left's sympathy for the strikers and opposition to government policy. The 'Shrewsbury Two' were imprisoned for violence and intimidation during an industrial dispute under a Labour Government whose Home Secretary made no attempt to overturn the court's verdict. All these examples cast doubt on the view that Thatcherism has introduced a 'strong state' to replace a 'liberal state'. If Britain does have a strong state, which is most doubtful in this author's view, then it predates Mrs Thatcher's 1979 election victory.

It may be argued that Thatcherism has shown little interest in either governmental institutional reform or the concept of state power beyond the provision of defence and law and order. Mrs Thatcher has refused to reform the civil service along the lines of politicisation suggested by John Hoskyns; she has no interest in electoral reform or devolution, and notions of a united states of Europe as a third superpower have never concerned her. Local government reform, such as the abolition of the GLC and Metropolitan counties, has been a by-product of her revulsion at high levels of public spending, rather than to achieve administrative modernisation. House of Lords reform, Bills of Right proposals, or the creation of a Department for the Opposition, as suggested by Sir Douglas Wass, have also been ignored. Although such political and constitutional reform has been on the agenda for many years, Mrs Thatcher and the Thatcherites have little time for it. The main reason is that it is not economic. It does not help to destroy socialism and promote the market economy, which is at the centre of Thatcherite ideology. Potential reform of the BBC, for example, reached the Thatcherite agenda only because of the great potentiality for expanding the free-market in broadcasting. Thatcherism has shown itself, above all, to be an economic ideology which utilises political methods and institutions to its own purpose. Public policy is consequently judged according to its ability to further the cause of a more market-oriented, dynamic, and meritocratic society. Thatcherism is both pure ideology and radical populism.

The targets of Thatcherism have been the pillars of post-war consensus, but true though this is it is not the whole truth. A substantial body of recent literature already exists on the nature of the post-1945 'Butskellite' consensus and the extent of Mrs Thatcher's repudiation of it. Indeed, much of the literature has approached the subject through an analysis of aspects of Thatcherism. Dennis Kavanagh's stimulating study argued that 'by the early 1950's it was already possible to refer to a post-war consensus on many, though not all, policies'.[21] He cites not only decolonisation and NATO membership in foreign affairs, but full-employment budgets, public ownership of basic services, greater acceptance of trade unions and an increased public sector implying a reduced role for the market. Most authors, including this one, are in broad agreement with this definition.

Disagreement has hitherto arisen over the nature and success of the Thatcherite challenge since 1979. Peter Jenkins, while critical of aspects of the consensus, believes it to be preferable to Thatcherism based, as he understands it, on a conspiracy theory which grotesquely magnifies the post-1945 policy blemishes.[22] By contrast, John Vincent has argued that Mrs Thatcher has not essentially changed very much, administering the inheritance left by Attlee except in marginal areas like privatisation.[23]

This account, however, intends to cut across this familiar analysis. My contention is that the post-war consensus existed largely in name only from 1945 to 1972 and was pursued to its logical conclusion – with disastrous consequences – from 1972 until the IMF crisis of 1976. Taking the five most accepted domestic areas of the consensus – Welfarism, trade-union power, national-isation, public sector anti-market sentiment, and Keynesian macro-economic management to prevent unemployment – it transpires that action does not match the political rhetoric until the post-Selsdon man Heath U-turns.[24]

Firstly it may be argued that the Welfare State pre-dated the Attlee government in any case. Welfarism has a long history going back to the Tudor Poor Law reforms of 1536 and 1601 and in the 20th century, manifested itself with the pre-First World War innovations. The Attlee administration extended the Welfare State, but not as much as has since been claimed by its protagon-ists. Means testing, after all, led to the famous (or infamous) resignation of Nye Bevan, John Freeman and Harold Wilson after the April 1951 budget. To be sure, the growth of the Welfare State continued, albeit at a slow pace, in the 1950s and 1960s, but it was not until the public spending boom of the Heath period that Welfare spending started to accelerate appreciably. The welfare 'burden', based on the extension of the principle of universality to groups such as the over-80s and single parent families, then began to increase. Moreover, between 1970 and 1974, the basic pension was increased by 55 per cent and the £10 Christmas bonus introduced. Labour continued such policies as part of the social wage input to the Social Contract after returning to power in 1974. Only after the 1970s did the cost of the Welfare State, rather than its social objectives, force itself on to the political agenda.

Secondly, trade-union power and the associated question of 'who rules?' was manifested infrequently before the Heath period. Peter Hain has argued, with some justification, that the trade unions were faced with persistent hostility by governments of all parties in the post-war era.[25] Attlee used troops to break the dock strike; Wilson attacked the communist element in the 1966 seamen's dispute. Despite inclusion in frequent discussions with the government over incomes policy, the unions invariably found themselves in a defensive political stance resisting wage control where they could. But the post-1972 Heath government changed all that. The unions were brought within the policy process as never before, establishing themselves as central pillars of the corporate state. But equally, their propensity to use industrial action increased, providing a series of industrial victories, the most spectacular of which were the 1972 and 1974 miners' strikes. Heath, trapped by the logic of his own corporate state, was unwilling either to use troops or the police to defeat the miners, or to fight a candlelit confrontation election in February 1974. Tripartism had elevated the union leaders to a higher political level than Cabinet ministers. Heath's consensual appeasement of union power elevated those, like Arthur Scargill, who sought industrial victories through the strength of the flying picket. Labour's Social Contract compounded the process until reality began to dawn as the IMF crisis developed.

Thirdly, nationalisation of basic or monopoly industries, while a feature of the Attlee period, was not central to the economic policies of either party in the consensus era. The Churchill Government denationalised steel; Gaitskell sought to remove Clause IV from the Labour Party's constitution; Wilson faced backbench Labour opposition to steel renationalisation and was loath to nationalise much else; and public opinion was hostile to further nationalisation reflected by Croslandite revisionism in Labour's policy making elite. Moreover the existing nationalised industries were almost run on market lines. White Papers under both Conservative and Labour governments in the 1960s stressed efficiency, marginal cost pricing, breaking even and the avoidance of financial deficits. Indeed, financial targets were explicitly encouraged.

Again it was the Heath Government which disrupted the
pattern. Heath extended both formal and back-door nationalisation. Rolls-Royce, Upper Clyde Shipbuilders, Meriden Motor-
cycles and the highly interventionist 1972 Industry Act speeded up
the stroll of state control into a forced march. Simultaneously,
Heath scrapped the financial targets for nationalised industries in
the vain and illusory pursuit of price control, culminating in both
chronic nationalised industry deficits and accelerating inflation.
Nationalised industry losses were simply written off, new investment in the coal industry reversed the Labour policy of running
the industry down, regional policy went beyond anything of the
Wilson era, and a massive 'modernisation' programme for British
Steel provided crippling losses for the Callaghan and Thatcher
governments. As Andrew Roth put it, Mr Heath 'began donning,
slightly dyed, the industrial aid garments of the hated Harold
Wilson'.[26]

But politically Heath went further than Wilson. Before Heath,
nationalisation had been associated only with the Labour Party or,
more specifically, with the left-wing. Heath gave nationalisation a
political legitimacy in the 1970s which it had never acquired in
economic terms and which now cut away the ground from under
the Labour moderates. Nationalisation of hundreds of companies
was postulated by the 1973 Labour conference and Wilson was
embarked on a battle with the pro-nationalisation left which was
settled in Wilson's favour only with Tony Benn's demotion from
Industry to Energy in the wake of the 1975 EEC referendum. Far
from being a central feature of the post- war consensus, nationalisation was in retreat until Heath revived it and with it, the Labour
left's devotion to Clause IV.

Fourthly, Keynesian economics to pursue full employment was
only sporadically tried in the post-war period; again, it was the
Heath Government which wholeheartedly and unreservedly
embraced it after 1972. Until the floating of the pound in June
1972, the balance of payments constraints limited Keynesian
expansion aims to brief periods of 'go' followed by longer periods
of 'stop'. To be sure, some Chancellors sought ways of breaking
free but never succeeded. R. A. Butler's ROBOT plan in 1952 –
now extensively documented by protagonists and opponents alike
– foundered on Churchill's commitment to preserve the Bretton
Woods international financial system.[27] Reggie Maudlings's 1964

expansion ended in the first few hours of the 1964–6 Wilson Government. Nor was the establishment commitment to Keynesianism unequivocal, as the resignation of Thorneycroft, Birch and Powell in 1958 over a trivial £50 million public overspend demonstrated.

Labour Governments were if anything more deflationary than Conservative ones. Cripps's austerity, Jim Callaghan's July 1966 measures and Roy Jenkins's 1969–70 budget surplus were motivated by considerations quite different from accepted Keynesianism. It was the Heath government which embraced Keynesian nostrums unrestrained by balance of payment considerations. The Jenkins budget surplus was transformed into a £4 billion deficit (in 1973 money terms) in three and a half years. Monetary policy was loosened to an extent unknown before; the raising of interest rates was rejected as damaging to the 'growth' policy. Incomes policy controls – the other side of the Keynesian expansionary coin – were imposed in their strictest form since war-time rationing. Prices, incomes, profits and dividends were all statutorily controlled in a futile, yet damaging, attempt to stop inflation. As a result, economic dislocation and resource malappropriation existed along side an inflation which finally peaked at 27 per cent. Pure unreconstructed Keynesianism as pursued by Heath ended in disaster with the rate of unemployment higher in 1974 than when Heath took office in 1970. Labour continued the Keynesian approach for two years until the balance of payments, despite floating exchange rates, could no longer be ignored. Joel Barnett's elegant memoirs are a testament to dealing with Heath's Keynesian expansion and the legacy it created for the Labour Government.[28]

Fifthly and finally, the post-war consensus in favour of the public sector and hostile to the market, while evident after 1945, reached its peak only in the Heath period. The Attlee and Churchill Governments dismantled and then abolished war-time controls and rationing; the Heath Government gleefully issued ration cards (but stopped short of using them) during the energy crisis. Previous incomes policies had avoided penalising economic activity and output; the Heath controls were so comprehensive that market forces were severely undermined. Labour Governments, as opposed to the Labour left, had sought to reassure the private sector to encourage long-term investment. Heath gratuitously attacked the city and the 'unacceptable face of capitalism', the only memorable phrase of his premiership, even if a spectacular own goal. No government until 1972 so vilified the market as did Heath, in contradiction to the encouragement of a market economy which had featured so strongly in the 1970 Conservative manifesto.

In actuality, the post-war consensus on social and economic policy, discernable as it was in the reformist Attlee administration, was more rhetoric than substance in 1945–72. The consensus was really tried, and pushed to its logical conclusions with zeal, only after the 1972 Heath U-turns. Its effects in all areas were negative and damaging; its deliverance came first from Jim Callaghan in 1976 and then from Margaret Thatcher after 1979. The Thatcherite attack on the post-war consensus is real enough; but essentially it is an attack on the failures of the Conservative Party under Heath. For Thatcherism, 1975 is year zero when the Heath regime was overthrown. Not surprisingly, as will be discussed in Chapter 6, Thatcherism has engendered bitter and continuing controversy within the Conservative Party itself. In the view of this author, the ideological origins of Thatcherism lie in the trauma, failure and abject electoral defeat of the Conservative Party in 1970–4.

CHAPTER 2

The Scope of Thatcherism and Economic Policy

By the start of the second Thatcher government, the economic policy central to Thatcherite ideology had taken a decisive shape. Inflation had been reduced from 22 per cent to 4 per cent with the prospect that, give or take small fluctuations in its percentage rate, permanently low inflation would not be endangered by any Keynesian stimulus to inflate aggregate demand. One Cabinet dry when asked whether 4 per cent was still not too high, replied that '4 per cent is better than the 27 per cent Heath notched up. If you go for zero inflation you may end up with 2 per cent or −2 per cent. We just do not have the machinery to cope with prices coming down'.[1] The determination to reduce the PSBR had also been a hallmark of 1979–83, and the desirability of still further reductions was a view strongly held by Sir Geoffrey Howe's successor as Chancellor, Nigel Lawson. Tax cuts, deferred in the first term in the battle against inflation and excessive public spending, were also on the post-1983 economic agenda. Sustaining the recovery in production, output and growth which had been evident since 1981 was regarded as important in enabling the government to provide the climate for unemployment to be reduced from the 12–13 per cent level. As one backbench supporter of the government put it, 'The overall economic strategy was of course predetermined by the 1981 budget. Lawson's position as Chancellor became unchallengeable'.[2] The view of one prominent wet, while critical of 1979–83, was less critical of the post-1983 period:

> The Prime Minister and Chancellor, without publicly admitting it, effectively admitted that they made mistakes over exchange rate policy in 1980–81. The rise in the exchange rate did enormous damage but from 1983 onwards they recognised the

19

need to protect manufacturing industry without making it unnecessarily uncompetitive. We wets were saying that we must support British manufacturing industry. After 1983, manufacturing liquidity improved enormously and interest rates became less important and the buoyancy of profits made them reasonably peripheral.[3]

Furthermore, and equally as important, micro-economic reforms to stimulate self-employment, business start-ups, and a more entrepreneurial economy featured prominently in the government's plans. This chapter aims to examine the government's record in fulfilling these objectives within the context of Thatcherite ideology.

As far as overall macro-economic policy was concerned, the government was able to cut taxes – but not by the amount it would have preferred. It was able to reduce the PSBR – as low as £4 billion by the 1987 budget. But reducing public spending proved too difficult and the government resorted to holding the percentage level to GDP rather than cutting in real terms. The rate of economic growth remained remarkably high at, or around, the 3 per cent mark, contributing to rising living standards without provoking balance of payment crises. Unemployment continued to rise fitfully until a steady decline from mid-1986 reduced the aggregate total to under 3 million in the month after the 1987 General Election. Having topped 13.9 per cent, unemployment fell to 11.9 per cent by the end of the term of office.

The details of such policy outcomes reveal similar political battles in Cabinet, parliament and the economic policy machine as existed in the first term. Chancellor Lawson, with some justification, regarded himself as fighting a beleaguered battle against a range of forces hoping to divert his policy from his stated goals. On entering 11 Downing Street, Mr Lawson inherited the lowest level of inflation, 3.7 per cent, for fifteen years, and economic growth averaging a stunning 4 per cent over the previous six months. In the 1983 Queen's speech, he reiterated commitments to rigorous control of public sector borrowing as an essential ingredient to provide the balance between fiscal and monetary policy. This would entail a firm control of public spending without which he could not promise tax cuts in the lifetime of the parliament. There would be no scope for relaxing public spending control in 1983 or in any other year. Within a month, Mr Lawson's determination to restrict the growth in public spending, and to offend colleagues in spending departments, was graphically illustrated by the Chancellor's disclosures that an £877.5 million public spending overrun demanded further restrictions. A £500 million emergency package was agreed by the Cabinet on 7 July, involving cuts – or rather limits on the rate of increase – in spending on Defence (£240 million), Employment (£25.3 million), Education (£36 million), Health (£140 million), and Transport (£16 million). Moreover, on July 21, the Cabinet further agreed to trim future spending programmes by £5 billion in order to hold the total public spending figure at £126.4 billion. The government was to find that holding public spending to planned levels was to be categorised as 'cuts' – with politically damaging implications of 'uncaring' neglect of public services such as Health and Education.

The key dilemma the government faced was that there was little possibility of the promised tax cuts if public spending could not be controlled. But the greater the political viability of controlling public spending, the greater the outcry to increase that same spending from lobby groups and from the Conservative left. This problem dogged the government throughout 1983–7. In July 1983, for example, Mrs Thatcher doubted whether taxes would be cut in the 1984 budget – this was a task for the lifetime of the parliament. Referring to the 'demand led' nature of much social service spending she admitted that, with more pensioners and social security claimants, there was a long-term problem of public spending because of its natural tendency to rise. Similarly, Mr Lawson argued that, as public spending was threatening to rise more quickly than economic growth,

either taxation will have to go up or we have got to find savings in public expenditure. If we put taxation up, then this is going to damage the prospects for growth in the economy over the longer term and it is that growth in the economy in the longer term which is the only way in which we can afford the better public services which we want to see. We have got to look at a number of things which may be, in some people's eyes, sacred cows, and we have got to find the most sensible way of making the savings which will enable us not merely to prevent taxation from rising, but enable taxation to be reduced.[4]

Although Mr Lawson was ultimately able to reduce taxation, this owed as much to buoyant Treasury revenues as to public expenditure restraint, let alone actual real cuts. The November 1983 Public Expenditure statement thus aimed at holding spending at the £126.4 billion figure of the 1983 White Paper while increasing revenue by £1.9 billion from privatisation proceeds. Even so, a 1 per cent rise in NHS spending was announced, an extra £422 million for agricultural subsidies, and higher national insurance charges on those on over £12,220 per annum income. The public expenditure plans estimated that agricultural support subsidies would total £2.2 billion, outspending the Departments of Trade and Industry, and Energy put together.[5] Such subsidies, running contrary to the government's free market ideology indicated the difficulty in controlling demand led (or EEC led) expenditure.

The public spending dilemma continued in the immediate run-up to the 1984 budget. In February Peter Rees, the Chief Secretary to the Treasury, announced in the Public Spending White Paper that the level of spending was expected to remain broadly unchanged until 1986–7, allowing tax cuts provided economic growth was sustained. The prospect of actually cutting public spending had been implicitly abandoned. Thus 1985–6 expenditure was planned to rise 4.5 per cent to £132.1 billion and in 1986–7 by 3.5 per cent to £136.7 billion. However, such figures would represent a fall from 43 per cent to 40 per cent of GDP, just below the level the government had inherited in 1979.[6]

The March 1984 budget itself was more radical than had been suggested by the public expenditure battles. Announcing a substantial cut in income tax for the coming year, the Chancellor held out the prospect of more reductions in 1985 and in subsequent years, provided public spending was held in check. Within the confines of a broadly neutral budget which left total revenues little changed, Mr Lawson redistributed the tax burden between groups of taxpayers. A 12.5 per cent increase in the basic income tax threshold, 7 per cent more than necessary to compensate for inflation, was largely financed by extending VAT to building alterations and hot take-away food and raising excise duties on drink, tobacco, petrol and vehicle licences. Mr Lawson emphasised the help the higher tax thresholds would give the low paid, 850,000 of whom would be taken out of the tax net. He said the switch from income to spending taxes would improve incentives and increase freedom of choice. For savers, Mr Lawson abolished the surcharge on substantial investment incomes and reduced stamp duty on share deals and home sales.

The budget also envisaged a PSBR reduction from £10 billion to £7.25 billion in 1984–5. A £7 billion PSBR was projected up to 1988–9 but by March 1987 Mr Lawson announced a £4 billion PSBR, a considerable achievement given the pressure for further tax cuts and the clamouring for increased public spending in areas of political sensitivity. One Cabinet Minister, not noted for dry economic views, thought that 'In the first term there was too much emphasis on the PSBR. But in the second term, I think everyone was happier. The Grantham Housewife view of not borrowing more than you have to is immensely valuable'.[7] Another notable feature of the 1984 budget was to attempt to switch taxation from direct to indirect to encourage incentives. This had long been a Thatcherite aim and, indeed, can be traced back to Mr Heath's Selsdon period prior to the 1970 Election. As Mr Lawson put it:

> The broad principle was clearly set out in the manifesto on which we were first elected in 1979. This emphasised the need for a switch from taxes on earnings to taxes on spending. My predecessor made an important move in this direction in his first budget, and the time has come to make a further move today. To reduce direct taxation by this means is important in two ways. It improves incentives and makes it more worth while to work, and it increases the freedom of choice of the individual. . . Changes in excise duties will, all told, bring in some £840m in 1984–5, some £200m more than is required to keep pace with inflation. The addition is of course due to the increase in tobacco duty.[8]

Overall, the 1984 budget could be described as the most Thatcherite hitherto. However, it was still the case after the budget that 9p off the standard rate of income tax would have been required to reduce the tax burden for a couple on average earnings to its 1978–9 level. Tax cuts, therefore, continued to be a high priority for the Chancellor.

The November 1984 economic statement bore this out. Tax cuts of £1.5 billion were anticipated for 1985 following the Cabinet's decision to keep 1985–6 public spending at a total of £132 billion, albeit £300 million more than the target set in March 1984. However, a 3.5 per cent growth rate indicated increased Treasury revenues giving Mr Lawson extra scope. Such optimism was particularly impressive as the miners' strike was by then seven months underway. But it was not to last. In January, as the pound fell against the dollar suggesting the possibility of a parity rate, two increases in interest rates followed and the Chancellor bemoaned that expected tax cuts were jeopardised. Although there was little evidence of an economic crisis or a collapse of sterling, and although a lower pound was helping exports, a political panic developed, only partly at the instigation of Shadow Chancellor, Roy Hattersley, which led the government to intervene on sterling's behalf. On 29 January 1985, a 2 per cent increase in base rates was seen as justified to avoid any misconception of the government's resolve to conquer inflation. The anxieties over sterling, however, as Mr Lawson told the Treasury Select Committee, were overdone. By March, the pound was appreciating quickly and on 15 April surged to a seven-month high against the dollar. Within two years, the rate was almost $1.70 to £1, and the familiar fears of exporters losing competitiveness were being expressed. The January 1985 'crisis' turned out to have been no such thing. As Peter Browning has noted, the 1967 devaluation had caused ugly crowds to gather in Downing Street,[9] but the 1984–5 depreciation, which amounted to 20 per cent during the year, went almost unheralded.

Subsequently, however, as the pound appreciated between 1985 and 1987, the CBI, despite occasional misgivings, did not indulge in the sort of public castigation of the government which had featured in the first term. One junior minister recalled that 'the CBI were very buoyant – previously they had been depressed. Instead of complaining about whatever was flavour of the month, often the exchange rate, they were eager to come to government to ask how to help'.[10]

Undoubtedly, though, the perceived damage to the government's macro-economic strategy did limit the Chancellor's radicalism in the March 1985 budget. Modest tax cuts of only £730 million were made possible by increasing tax allowances more than the rate of inflation; the self-employed received relief with their heavy National Insurance contributions; Capital Gains tax was reformed at a cost of £155 million per annum; 15 stamp duties abolished;

taxes on alcohol, tobacco and motoring increased; and the PSBR pegged at £7 billion in line with previous forecasts. Despite the increases in interest rates, economic growth was 3.5 per cent, and inflation expected to increase to 6 per cent because the depreciation of sterling had pushed up import costs. Reflecting the growing concern with the Conservative Party on the unemployment issue, Mr Lawson had stated that:

Looking ahead, we are now about to embark on what will be the fifth successive year of steady growth, with output in 1985 as a whole set to rise by a further 3.5%. Inflation may edge up for a time, perhaps to 6% by the middle of the year, but should then fall back to 5% by the end of the year and lower still in 1986. While there can be no disputing the strength and durability of the economic upswing, there is equally no disputing the fact that it is marred by an unacceptably high level of unemployment. And this despite the fact that the latest figures suggest that employment has risen by half a million over the past two years, with a further increase likely over the year ahead. The Government has therefore decided to promote a substantial expansion of the Youth Training Scheme. Provided employers contribute a major share of the cost, the Government is prepared to provide further funds to launch this new initiative, over and above the existing £800 million a year of public expenditure on the YTS. The expanded scheme would offer places lasting two years for 16-year-old and one year for 17-year-old school-leavers, leading to a recognised qualification... In addition, Mr Tom King will be issuing a consultative document about the future of the Wages Councils later this week. Wages Councils destroy jobs by making it illegal for employers to offer work at wages they can afford and the unemployed are prepared to accept. This applies in particular to small employers and to youngsters looking for their first job. The document will cover a number of proposals for radical change, including complete abolition.[11]

The 1985 budget, with its background of the costs of the miners' dispute, the interest rate increases following the January sterling crisis, and the forecast increase in the inflation rate to 6 per cent, was as Thatcherite as it could be. Above all, it showed the difficulty of macro-economic planning with any certainty from one year to the next. According to Grahame Thompson, the 1985 budget 'confirmed the idea that orthodox annual budgets as such – i.e. in terms of altering government expenditure levels – have been losing their significance under Conservative administrations'. [12] Although Thompson bemoans the passing of the regulatory 'demand management' budget, he should not be surprised at the greater supply side emphasis that was a marked feature of the 1985 budget. The days of Barber or Healey-style mini-budgets were clearly over.

Political considerations also affected economic options in 1985. Following the Brecon and Radnor by-election defeat on 4 July, where the Conservatives came third, there was a widespread belief that the government had cut public spending, causing hardship, unemployment and a neglect of the Health Service. A campaign developed across party lines to defer tax cuts in favour of public spending increases which allegedly would reduce unemployment more effectively. Excess spending bids from the departments were more difficult for the Treasury to resist even with a £6 billion contingency reserve. Despite increased spending in real terms, a gallup poll in July 1985 discovered that 76 per cent of respondents thought there had been too little spent on the NHS and 74 per cent considered education spending inadequate. [13]

The reality was that Thatcherism was not actually cutting public spending at all; it was merely restricting its rate of increase, and that with great difficulty, as the Cabinet battles and Star Chamber deliberations testified. One Cabinet minister recalled that 'I favoured not increasing public spending; if you go down that road, it is a primrose path to perdition'. [14] However, as Table 2.1 below indicates, most programmes had witnessed considerable increases in spending levels.

In terms of Thatcherite ideology, the 'failure' actually to cut public expenditure resulted not from political will but from the demand led nature of much spending. The failure of the Fowler review of Social Security spending to reduce the aggregate total by more than £750 million out of £36 billion, illustrates this well. Thus, as one study of social security expenditure put it, 'if recent trends continue and unless unemployment is distinctly lower in the immediate future, which the government itself does not anticipate, or there are cuts in the real value of benefits, it seems possible that social security expenditure may again overshoot [spending]

TABLE 2.1   Changes in public expenditure in real terms, 1979/80
to 1984/85

All figures in £ million	1979/80 outturn	1984/85 estimated outturn	Increase from 1970/80 to 1984/85
Defence	13,405	16,467	+22.8%
Education and Science	12,994	13,125	+ 1.0%
Health	12,933	15,087	+16.7%
Social Security	28,204	36,221	+28.4%
Industry, Energy, Trade and Employment	5,822	6,856	+17.8%
Housing	6,569	2.979	−54.6%
Other Environmental services	3,833	3,592	− 6.3%
Law, Order and protective services	3,746	4,837	+29.1%
Scotland	6,613	6,817	+ 3.1%
Northern Ireland	3,615	3,875	+ 7.2%
1983/84 price base			

Source: The Government Expenditure Plans

targets'.[15] One Cabinet minister considered that 'Fowler fudged
the reform – he did not believe in the black economy earnings'[16]
and another Cabinet minister confessed that 'The social security
reforms were less far reaching than some would have hoped'.[17]
And one Health minister admitted that 'The Fowler Review could
have saved more money – we could have means tested child
benefit. But he diminished the poverty trap and targeted benefits
into a better structure'.[18]

Similarly, EEC determined agricultural spending, mortgage
interest tax relief rising from £1 billion to £4 billion and the
increased cost of pensions, all limited the government's room for
manoeuvre without a full re-assessment of priorities. Such a course
of action would have challenged universality of welfare benefits by
introducing means testing, a policy that Thatcherites privately
favoured but politically shrank from – at least in the 1983–7
context.

Viewed in these terms, it is not surprising that Mrs Thatcher was
regarded as achieving a political victory after Cabinet, in November 1985, agreed to freeze – not cut – public spending for three
years. The Cabinet meeting passed off smoothly. The Treasury

had earlier struck deals with the major departments. Ministers praised Mr John MacGregor, who became Chief Secretary to the Treasury in the September reshuffle, for his handling of his first public spending round. Lord Whitelaw's 'star chamber' succeeded in settling most of the differences, although this was helped by the Treasury's room for manoeuvre with a large reserve and extra privatisation receipts ahead.

In the autumn statement Mr Lawson expected extra public spending totalling £5 billion over two years to be paid for by doubling the rate at which state assets would be sold to the public. Public spending totals for 1986–7 and 1987–8 remained at the forecast £139 billion and £144 billion respectively. The Chancellor, however, insisted that even if asset sales were excluded from the calculation, public spending could be shown to be under control. It was 'broadly flat' in real terms and falling from 45 per cent of national income in 1985 to only 42 per cent by 1988–9. But, as in 1985, optimism over tax cuts again proved over optimistic. The dramatic fall in oil prices, from roughly $30 to $10 per barrel, significantly reduced oil revenues to the Treasury and limited the scope for tax reductions. As Mr Lawson told the Commons on 13 February 1986:

> It would be highly desirable and beneficial for the British economy and beneficial for employment if we could reduce the burden of taxation generally and of income tax in particular. But the plain fact is that the substantial loss of North Sea Oil revenues as a result of the sharp fall in the oil price is not an excuse; it is a fact.[19]

Each dollar fall in the price of oil on a stable exchange rate cost the Treasury £500 million in lost revenue in the months immediately preceding the 1986 budget.

Nevertheless, the Chancellor again produced as Thatcherite a budget as such circumstances permitted. Income tax was cut from 30 per cent to 29 per cent. To encourage 'people's capitalism', the Personal Equity Plan (PEP) provided tax incentives to encourage individuals to invest in the British stock market. Confirming that North Sea Oil revenues had been halved to £6 billion, he was still able to maintain a £7 billion PSBR. Even taxes on alcohol were unaffected and the road fund licence unchanged. In total the revenue costs of the budget were £815 million above the cost of indexation. The main political attack centred on the lack of any reflation to reduce unemployment and despite the income tax cut, opinion polls showed the budget to be marginally unpopular. How far this reaction was a legacy of general government unpopularity following the Westland crisis in January 1986 is open to conjecture but by April 1986 Labour was twelve points ahead of the Conservatives in one poll. The sterling crisis had constrained the 1985 budget and the oil price fall had partially de-radicalised the 1986 budget. With the government behind in the polls, the Chancellor's macro-economic strategy had, at most, only two more budgets left to rectify the political situation.

From mid-1986, however, the situation improved for the government. Within just one year, the Chancellor was being described as 'Lucky Lawson'. The recovery had proved sustainable with output rising. The rate of growth at over 3 per cent was the highest in the EEC. Treasury revenues were buoyant, aided by high consumer spending, boosting VAT receipts. Oil prices started to creep upwards, unemployment started to fall (albeit gradually), and Corporation Tax revenue increased with corporate profit growth. In Autumn 1986, Mr Lawson was able to announce public spending increases in the politically vulnerable areas of Health and Education, 'without adding a penny piece to the borrowing requirement'. Public expenditure plans showed significant increases in most areas. Spending for 1987–8 was planned to be £7.5 billion higher than implied at the time of the 1986 budget. The Chancellor of the Exchequer disclosed that the government had failed to control public spending, in spite of the advantage of lower-than-expected inflation. The public spending planning total was put at £140.4 billion for the current year, £1.3 billion up on the original target. However, the main increases were for the later years. The planning total for 1987–8 was targeted at £148.6 billion, compared with £143.9 billion at budget time. In addition, the Chancellor reduced the reserve from £6.3 billion to £3.5 billion and added an extra £250 million to sales of state assets. Those three changes amounted to an additional £7.5 billion of spending. There was an extra £1.7 billion on social security, £2.2 billion on Education, £630 million for Health and £460 million for the Department of Energy. In the following year, 1988–9, the planning total for public spending was raised by £5.5 billion to £154.2

billion and in 1989–90 the target is £161.5 billion. The Chancellor justified this by the buoyancy of non-oil tax revenues, expected to be £2 billion higher than originally estimated, and by the fact that public spending was forecast to decline as a proportion of GDP.

In the 1987 budget, income tax was cut from 29 per cent to 27 per cent and the PSBR reduced from £7 billion to £4 billion. Nigel Lawson boasted of a hat-trick of reduced taxes, a falling PSBR, and increased social spending. The 1987 budget was also presented as prudent by limiting the tax cut to 2 per cent in order to reduce borrowing and interest rates. The government's fear that a tax-cutting budget would be portrayed by the opposition as vote-buying irresponsibility was thus avoided. One backbench wet, discussing the Chancellor's policies, noted that 'The longer he stayed in the job, the more impressive he became. Complacency became confidence. But I am disappointed we did not do more on raising tax thresholds and I am also in favour of differential rates to help the low paid. We were unfairly castigated as an uncaring party when we were giving a wide number of benefits to so many people'.[20] But an economist, clearly unsympathetic to Thatcherism, Grahame Thompson, has rightly argued that 'the technical details of this or that particular mechanism for regulating the economy misses the point of the politically and ideologically motivated attack on all things collective and socialistic. Here the Tories have changed, or are changing, the terrain on which the very terms of economic debate can take place, and with it, the characteristic practices of the economy itself'.[21] The 1987 budget in particular, demonstrated this approach.

Mr Kinnock's allegation that it was a 'bribes budget', and that the Chancellor should have used available resources to stimulate investment, cure unemployment, build houses and develop industry, while effective as parliamentary rhetoric, was unlikely to convince an electorate which regarded its own prosperity as paramount. In this way, the social wage arguments which Labour had successfully fostered between the two 1974 elections had been replaced by an individualistic approach to the economy in keeping with Thatcherite ideology. When this was also buttressed by spending increases in socially sensitive areas, Labour's attack was doubly blunted. Mr Lawson's announcement of tax cuts was thus couched in the long-term framework of Thatcherism:

In my Budget speech last year, I reaffirmed the aim, set out by my predecessor in 1979, to reduce the basic rate of income tax to no more than 25 per cent. That remains my firm objective. However, given my decision to use the greater part of the fiscal scope I now have to reduce the public sector borrowing requirement, that goal cannot be achieved in this Budget. I can, however, take a further step towards it, as I did last year. I am therefore reducing the basic rate of income tax by 2p, to 27 per cent. This reduction, which will benefit every taxpayer in the land, will be worth more than £3 a week to a man on average earnings. There will, of course, be a consequential reduction in the rate of advance corporation tax, and – as last year – I also propose a corresponding cut in the small companies' rate of corporation tax from 29 per cent to 27 per cent. Taken together with the income tax change, this will mean a significant reduction in the tax burden on small businesses, which are so important for future growth and jobs.[22]

In overall terms, the 1983–7 economic strategy was consistent with Thatcherite ideology and, given the existing economic circumstances outside the government's control, was as radical as could be expected. Low inflation, sustained recovery, a high growth rate, falling taxes, drastically reduced borrowing and a balance of payments surplus was an impressive record. On the debit side, the failure actually to cut public spending clearly blunted the radical edge of economic reform, and the existence of some areas of public spending operated counter to free-market principles. The market distortions of mortgage interest tax relief and the over-generous tax status of the pensions industry might just be defended in terms of electoral necessity. As one backbench MP described mortgage interest relief, 'There is no economic justification for it at all but it would take great courage to get rid of it as there are more mortgages and more up to the £30,000 limit'.[23] But the failure to reduce the £2 to £3 billion spent annually on agricultural subsidy – aside from the added burden of £13 per week per household in higher food prices – is indefensible. Pleading EEC pressure is no excuse for the subsidisation of agriculture with all the attendant woes of surpluses, storing, and dumping on world markets. The government would not have dreamed of treating coal, steel, BL, British Rail and other still nationalised industries in the way that it has treated agriculture to ever-increasing and often open-ended subsidies. Conservative opponents of such an essentially socialist agricultural subsidy system, such as Teddy Taylor and Richard Body,[24] have long been known to enjoy the support of Mrs Thatcher and the more radical Thatcherite ministers in private. Indeed, the Treasury's own *Economic Progress Report*, quoting with approval Nigel Lawson's hostility to worldwide agricultural protectionism, castigated the follies of the CAP: 'The net result', the Treasury argued 'is that national output is produced less efficiently and consumers are worse off'.[25] But would reform be 'politically' feasible? Recent evidence suggests that the deferment of the repatriation of agricultural policy to the British government and away from the EEC is much less risky politically than has been thought.[26] Moreover, the benefits to the consumer of market prices for food would also certainly outweigh any lost agricultural votes. CAP reform was a reform tragically and unnecessarily passed by in 1983–7. Similarly, Welfare State spending, an area of considerable electoral susceptibility, also proved beyond the reach of public spending discipline because of the demand led nature of its component parts.

As in the first Thatcher term, the question of unemployment proved the greatest political embarrassment to the government's economic strategy. Far from deliberately creating unemployment, as academic economists on the left, such as MacInnes[27] have claimed, the Thatcher Governments have constantly feared the electoral impact of high unemployment, and especially persisting unemployment. The Thatcherite approach to the problem has been essentially a micro-economic one, eschewing Keynesian nostrums of artificially increasing aggregate demand. Without rehearsing familiar arguments pointing out the failure of Keynesian remedies in Britain,[28] the second Thatcher Government proved more willing to embark upon labour-market reforms, business deregulation and the encouragement of incentives to work. The process was a difficult and long-term one, accompanied by considerable political and public disquiet. During the first Thatcher term, ministers had consistently refused to take the blame for rising unemployment, and while the new Employment Secretary, Tom King, officially did so in 1983, he seemed much more defensive than his predecessors, conveying an impression that government inactivity was partly responsible for human misery. King's media style lacked the abrasiveness of his immediate predecessor, Norman Tebbit, and contributed to the government looking guilty when each set of unemployment figures was announced. The increase in the numbers at work, first evident in February 1984, which indicated a trend towards the employment of a larger proportion of the workforce, was treated as low key and rarely deployed as an argument to suggest the unemployment situation was more complicated than the gross total indicated.

Similarly, the re-structuring of the British economy away from manufacturing and towards services – an inevitable and desirable process to maximise Britain's international comparative advantage – was lamely lamented by the government for too long during the 1983–5 period. A more robust analysis would have explained the paradox of an economy growing at 3 per cent, but unemployment remaining virtually static at over 3 million. For example, the relative importance of services has been increasing in all industrial economies, though it has reached its furthest development in the United States. Services now account for three-quarters of non-agricultural employment in the United States compared with about 60 per cent in Britain. The pattern in Britain was similar. The number of jobs in service industries, (including the self-employed, two-thirds of whom work in services) had risen by 1.25 million over the previous ten years. Employment in professional and scientific services (mostly education and health) increased by half a million, followed by 'miscellaneous' services (sport and leisure, restaurants, clubs and pubs, as well as many computer-based services) and insurance, banking, finance and business services.

The number of service jobs had scarcely been dented by the recession at a time when manufacturing employment had shrunk by a quarter. The picture had also been changed by the Employment Department's discovery of nearly 900,000 extra workers – mostly in services – missed from previous industry surveys. Service employment had been rising since the beginning of 1983, while the total number of those in work (including the self-employed) in all industries and services began to edge up in the spring. In short, the increase in service jobs between 1973 and 1983 was swamped by a huge decline in manufacturing employment. As a result, the total number of jobs in the economy fell by 1.5 million. One lesson drawn from American experience concerns labour flexibility.

Workers in the United States change jobs more than twice as often
as in Britain, they are more ready to move to where the jobs are,
and they have been willing to accept lower wages. Real hourly
earnings, adjusted for the rise in the cost of living, fell during the
1970s; in Britain, they rose steeply.

The government's failure to explain such economic facts of life
greatly contributed to the growth of the 'manufacturing-as-
priority' lobby, skilfully exploited by Labour and Alliance politicians. The public was led to believe, not that jobs came from
satisfied customers in all industries, service and manufacturing,
but that only an increase in manufacturing investment could
reduce unemployment. That such an analysis, quite contrary to
international trends and to the British evidence, should have
embarrassed the government is testimony to its failure to capture
the intellectual high ground on the employment debate. Political
discussion about the nature of unemployment rather than the gross
politically sensitive total was still comparatively rare. As Samuel
Brittan has noted, 'the most outstanding feature of the rise in
unemployment since 1980 is that the whole increase has been in
long-term jobless, out of work for more than a year. The number
unemployed for less has actually fallen. Transitional unemployment of two weeks or less is no higher than in 1975'.[29] The
government's failure to explain such realities hampered its case
with the public.

A shift in emphasis did occur, however, with the appointment of
David Young, formerly chairman of the Manpower Services
Commission (MSC), as a roving one-man think tank on job
creation and finally as Employment Secretary in September 1985.
Micro-economic measures to remove barriers to employment were
stressed. A White Paper in July 1985 concentrated on changes in
planning procedures to enable businesses to be established more
easily and the introduction of simplified planning zones in inner
cities operating on the lines of the enterprise zones pioneered by
Sir Geoffrey Howe. However, the greatest single boost to job
creation – the dismantling of the 1940s Green Belt system – was
specifically ruled out by both Lord Young and Environment
Secretary, Patrick Jenkin. The overclassification of agricultural
land by 1940s criteria thus continued greatly to restrict growth and
enterprise. A second White Paper, *Building Business not Barriers*,
was forthcoming in May 1986. It emphasised the government's

objective of cutting the dole queues by encouraging more small businesses to be started up and more self-employed and part-time workers. Among eighty proposals were a fairer VAT payment system, fewer planning regulations and less employment protection for workers in small firms. It also stated that civil servants may be faceless but should at least give their names when dealing with the public, and that tax and VAT men should visit companies together, rather than separately. Lord Young, announcing the White Paper in the Lords, said that it reflected 'our firm belief that only by removing barriers to business will enterprise flourish and the essential creation of wealth and jobs follow'.[30]

The government did decide, after much urging from free-market thinkers, to abolish wages councils for the under-21s, involving half a million workers. But again, this reform was muted. The Institute of Directors said the government had made a disappointing start to the battle to cut red tape. It should have had the courage of its convictions and abolished the councils altogether. Enterprise Allowances were also introduced to help the unemployed to become self-employed, even though more than 70 per cent of those starting businesses with the help of the government's £11 million Enterprise Allowance Scheme would have done so even if they had not had a state grant, according to a survey carried out for the Manpower Services Commission. The internal survey found that only 27 per cent of those asked would not have established their enterprise without the £1,000-a-year-grant paid under the scheme. A total of 42 per cent, however, said that they were encouraged to set up their businesses earlier because of the scheme. The survey found that an average of 24 full-time jobs and 44 part-time jobs were created for every 100 businesses started. 16 per cent of the firms expected to take on additional workers within the next six months. The report showed that 11 per cent of those who started small businesses under the scheme were women, while 72 per cent of businesses were operated by people aged between 18 and 44. The proportion of those entering the scheme who had been without a job for more than a year was 28 per cent.

The encouragement of self-employment was a marked feature of the second Thatcher term, although its job creation potential is by nature long-term as small businesses grow into large ones. In the 1970s, self-employment had fallen by 100,000, a catastrophic development for a 'capitalist' economy, but by 1987 had increased by 750,000. While such a trend augurs well for the Thatcherite enterprise economy, it did not provide the short-term solution to unemployment demanded by the government's critics. Nevertheless, the unemployment statistics did move in the government's favour eventually. October 1985 witnessed the biggest single fall for fourteen years and from July 1986, unemployment fell each month until the 1987 General Election. The fall in March 1987, for example, of 71,427 was the largest monthly fall since 1973 and prompted speculation about a general election. Unemployment was also falling in areas where it had been highest, with the largest relative drop in Wales. Although such falls were insufficient to bring the gross total below the politically sensitive 3 million mark, they did give some indication that the government's micro-economic approach was starting to have a beneficial effect. While in the view of this author, Britain's unemployment problem was a long-term one, originating in misplaced policies in 1945–79, it still remains the case that the second Thatcher Government was too slow and over-cautious in removing barriers to new jobs. A more determined approach would have involved a total reclassification of the Green Belt policy, the abolition of all wages councils, action against local authority penalisation of business, reform of the Rent Acts to encourage job mobility, greater increases in tax thresholds to eliminate the 'unemployment trap', an integrated tax and benefit system to encourage work incentives, elimination of employers' NIC and a further extension of the 1986 Restart Scheme to tackle long-term unemployment. Although there were some conspicuous bright spots, such as the growth of self-employment, the overall record in 1983–7 on employment matters was disappointing, given the Thatcherite emphasis on lower unemployment through micro-economic reform. But it must be noted that the appointment of Lord Young – assisted from September 1985 by Kenneth Clarke – did dramatically improve the political will to adopt more thoroughgoing Thatcherite solutions to the unemployment problem. Had Lord Young been appointed Employment Secretary in June 1983, the record would have been more encouraging. He brought a micro-economic reality to the sacred political cow of believing the aggregate unemployment figures. In Lord Young's view, 'The unemployment figures were phoney. We had allowed our society through 30 years of welfare state principles, to become distorted. Too much tax was taken from the low paid. None of my colleagues believed in the black economy. They did not think it existed. I went in for Restart and 10–15% went off the register just by being asked to fill out a form'.[31] The recognition of Britain's black economy by the political elite had finally begun.

CHAPTER 3

The Scope of Thatcherism and Trade-union Power

By the start of the second Thatcher term, the three pillars of trade-union power in 1945–79 had already been effectively demolished. The corporate state which involved trade unions directly in the Keynesian-inspired reflation plus incomes policy approach had been dismantled. Trade-union legal immunities had been significantly reduced by the 1980 and 1982 Employment Acts, which tackled the sensitive question of picketing and the closed shop. And Mrs Thatcher's determination to seek industrial victories in public-sector disputes had removed the greatest source of trade-union power – the almost inevitable government climbdown couched in the language of negotiation, compromise and consensus.

The 1983–7 Government continued to pursue these Thatcherite objectives. Although there was only one further Act limiting union legal powers, the 1984 Trade Union Act proved important, aiming specifically at removing unions' immunity to prosecution if a ballot had not been held to ratify strike action. The idea of this reform surfaced in Norman Tebbit's July 1983 White Paper, which proposed ballots of union members for the election of executives, ballots before strikes are called, and periodic votes among union memberships on whether political funds should be maintained. As Mr Tebbit explained to the Commons:

> The legislation will require elections to the governing bodies of trade unions to comply with the following principles – voting must be secret and by ballot paper; there must be an equal and unrestricted opportunity to vote; every union member should be able to cast his vote directly. These principles are not a legal straitjacket. They are the minimum necessary to ensure free,

fair and democratic elections. Within them, trade unions will be free to constitute their governing bodies in the way they judge will best serve their members' interests and to decide on the form of ballots. I also expect in due course to consult on the need for industrial relations in specific essential services to be governed by adequate procedure agreements, breach of which would deprive industrial action of immunity. I propose that the 1913 Act should be amended to require that political objectives and funds should be submitted to ballot at least every ten years. For some years there has been disquiet over the operation of the system for contracting out of the political levy. I therefore intend to invite the TUC to discuss the arrangements which trade unions themselves might take to ensure that their members are fully aware of their statutory rights and able to exercise them freely and effectively. I hope that the trade unions will be willing to take such steps. If that hope is disappointed, I would be ready to introduce measures, as we made clear in our manifesto, to guarantee a free and effective right of choice.[1]

Although the TUC ended its freeze on talks with Mr Tebbit, the discussions did not produce a government retreat and TUC leaders resolved to campaign against the legislation despite the likelihood of it reaching the statute book. Bill Keys, who led the TUC delegation, considered the proposals an 'utterly unwarranted interference in the rights of unions in a democratic society to govern themselves in the manner which their members have democratically chosen'. Nor did such objections dissuade Tom King, whose Bill published in October 1983 enshrined the July proposals. Part I of the Bill dealt with trade-union elections. Clause 1 required the executive to be elected by secret ballot of the union's members. Clause 1 provided that every person who has a vote or casting vote on this committee must owe his position to an election fulfilling the requirements in Clause 2 held within the last five years.

Clause 1 also provided that office holders in the union whose office gives them a vote or casting vote on the committee (such as the union's general secretary or president) must have been similarly elected to that office.

Clause 2 laid down that all elections to the principal executive committee of a trade union must comply with the following requirements. Entitlement to vote at the election must be accorded equally to all members of the union unless they are in certain listed groups, such as newly-joined or retired members, which are also excluded from voting under union rules. Voting in the election must be by the marking of a ballot paper and without interference or constraint. Those entitled to vote must, so far as is reasonably practicable, be supplied with a ballot paper and given a fair and convenient opportunity to vote in secret. Votes cast in the election must be fairly and accurately counted. No member is to be unreasonably prevented from standing for election, nor required to belong to a particular political party in order to do so.

Part II concentrated on the vital question of secret ballots before industrial action. Consequently, Clause 6 removed immunity from legal action in cases where trade unions do not hold a ballot before authorising or endorsing a call for a strike (or any other form of industrial action which interferes with, or breaks, the employment contracts of those called upon to take part in it). Clause 7 set out the requirements which strike ballots must satisfy. Entitlement to vote must be given to those, and only those, whom it is reasonable for the union to believe will be called upon to take or continue to take strike or other industrial action. Immunity will be lost if any member is called on to strike after being denied entitlement to vote.

Finally, Part III dealt with union political activities. The key Clause (9) provided that trade unions, which have in the past balloted their members, under the provisions of the Trade Union Act 1913, to enable them to spend money on political activities, must in future ballot their members at least every ten years if they wish to continue to do so. Clause 9 supplements the existing requirements in the 1913 Act, which govern the conduct of ballots on political funds.

The Bill became law in 1984 and, along with the 1980 and 1982 legislation, could claim to have restricted trade-union power to a reasonable degree as Thatcherism had intended. The legislation alone could not deliver industrial victories, as was demonstrated in the *Stockport Messenger* and Wapping disputes (or the use of the Common Law in the miners' strike), but it did provide employers with a weapon which could limit strike effectiveness.

In the *Stockport Messenger* dispute, where violent picketing and intimidation threatened to halt publication, the National Graphical

Association (NGA) initially refused to pay a fine of £50,000 imposed under the 1980 Act for illegal picketing. Hundreds of pickets besieged the *Stockport Messenger* plant in defiance of a threatened second injunction against the union after the High Court had granted an injunction restraining the NGA and the Court of Appeal had ordered seizure of the union's £10 million assets. Ultimately, the NGA was fined £525,000 for contempt of court in continuing the illegal picketing, and consequently found that financing the dispute was extremely onerous. Moreover, the TUC General Secretary, Len Murray, criticised the NGA's contempt of the law and secured TUC General Council support by 29 votes to 21. In his memoirs, Frank Chapple recalled that:

> The NGA's Joe Wade accused Murray and the TUC majority not only of selling his union down the river, but of sending the rest of the movement with them. It was the familiar lament of the union loser, anxious to shift the blame for defeat, but Murray had shown much-needed steel and heaved the whole trade union movement back from the edge of the precipice. It was a blow for moderation, struck while the Labour leader, Neil Kinnock, maintained an embarrassing silence in the face of inexcusable violence on the picket line.[2]

Now isolated, the NGA halted its mass picketing on 15 December 1983, and in January 1984 purged its contempt of court. The fines cost the union a total of £625,000 and Mr Eddie Shah emerged with an industrial victory after a six month dispute.

In the Wapping case, following Mr Rupert Murdoch's decision to move *The Times* and other newspapers from Gray's Inn Road to East London, the law also helped to weaken union power. Again, mass picketing of a violent and bitter nature occurred outside the 'Fortress Wapping' plant while EETPU members worked inside on new technology long opposed by traditional print unions. In February 1986, sequestration of the £17 million assets of the print union Sogat '82 was ordered in the High Court. Mr Justice Davies made the order after hearing that the union had ignored a court injunction ordering it to halt the blacking of News International's four national newspapers by members at wholesalers. The union, 4,000 of whose members were dismissed after going on strike, was also fined £25,000. But although the union, their NGA colleagues, and a regular army of left-wing pickets from varying walks of life, fought on for a year, Mr Murdoch, and the EETPU would not back down. Mass picketing, although declared illegal by the High Court in August 1986, continued almost as before. The two main print unions were ordered by Mr Justice Stuart-Smith to limit to six the number of their pickets outside the plant and at other premises owned by the company. The judge made the order after stating there was overwhelming evidence that employees who passed the pickets and daily demonstrators were almost invariably subjected to abuse and threats. There had been more sinister behaviour away from the plant. Some employees had been assaulted on joining or leaving company buses at pick-up or dropping off points. The Judge itemised individual cases of harrassment in which workers:

> have been followed, abused, threatened, put in fear and molested. Several have had their cars vandalized at home or had their houses daubed with the word 'scab'. One had a skip with four yards of earth, a wreath with the words 'in loving memory of X' (and then his name). Yet others have been rung at night, abused and threatened . . .
>
> Freedom of speech has never extended to intimidation, abuse and threats directed at those going about their lawful business.[3]

Probably the worst night of picket line violence occurred in January 1987 when police used horses as an alternative to deploying plastic bullets or CS gas. Deputy Assistant Commissioner Wyn Jones, in overall charge of police operations at Wapping, said the horses were called out because otherwise police would have suffered even worse injuries and risked being overrun. Although the government's legislation assisted News International, such police tactics – along with the co-operation of the EETPU and distributors of newspapers by road – enabled Mr Murdoch to win a significant industrial victory.

The winds of change blowing through Fleet Street might have dislodged trade-union opposition in any case; but with the legal weapon also available, the process was hastened. It is arguable that the threat of legal action prevented industrial disruption to the process, particularly at the *Financial Times* and *Daily Telegraph*. Moreover, the launching of *Today* with a no-strike deal with the

EETPU and Robert Maxwell's reorganisation at Mirror News-papers showed that the power of the print unions was no longer in terms of the veto on production that had once made them seemingly omnipotent. The threat of legal action, fines and sequestration played no small part in these events.

As far as the ballot provisions of the 1984 Act were concerned, there was again a clear change of political climate. Ballots proved popular with trade-union members and also with union leaders in the EETPU, AUEW and EMA. Balloting before a strike became the rule rather than the exception. However, balloting still produced votes in favour of industrial action by about 2:1. This may well indicate a smaller percentage for strike action than before the 1984 Act but it showed that ballots depended on the circumstances of the industry for their outcome. Philip Bassett has argued that there has been a further consequence:

what the figures fail to include is the change in attitude engendered by the 1984 Act's provision. Faced with well-known examples such as the London Underground workers' refusal to heed an unballoted strike call by the NUR in 1985, or the rejection of action by guards in the same union even after a ballot and on an issue – trains without guards – on which they had public sympathy, anecdotal evidence clearly suggests that the prospect of balloting (and obviously of losing) has restrained moves towards action that even in straitened times might otherwise have gone unchallenged.[4]

If Bassett is correct, the ballot provisions have tipped the balance much more against strike action than the 2:1 balloting figures reveal. In the case of the 1984 dock strike, for example, an anti-strike rebellion gained momentum after a ballot at Tilbury indicated a desire to return to work. A vote of 1,398 to 41 to return to work thus helped to end a strike in defiance of the union leadership, which rejected its outcome. Moreover, the TUC's decision not to expel unions that had defied General Council policy by accepting government money to conduct ballots – notably the EETPU and AUEW – indicated the political untenability of non-co-operation with popular legislation.

The effects also of a highly publicised decision not to strike, such as the NUR guards who voted 52 per cent to 48 per cent not to do so in August 1985, helped to push opinion within the union leadership against penalising unions who welcomed the ballot provisions of the 1984 Act. Indeed, one former union leader, Lord Chapple, has criticised the government for not going far enough. As he told the 1986 conference of the Institute of Directors:

> I support the present government's laws about balloting before strikes and for the election of union executives. My criticism of the Government is that it hasn't gone far enough. I've always thought that there should be secret postal balloting. For reasons which I've never understood, the Government has always been lukewarm about this.[5]

Similarly, the provisions of the 1984 Act relating to the election of union leaders has proved so popular that by 1987 the government was planning to extend them. The 1987 Conservative manifesto promised to introduce legislation to:

> ensure that all members of trade union governing bodies are elected by secret ballot at least once every five years; make independently supervised postal ballots compulsory for such elections; limit further the abuse of the closed shop by providing protection against unfair dismissal for all non-union employees, and removing any legal immunity from industrial action to establish or enforce a closed shop; provide new safeguards on the use of union funds, and establish a new trade union commissioner with the power to help individual trade unionists to enforce their fundamental rights.[6]

However, the government stopped well short of a concerted assault on free collective bargaining, itself identified as a source of unemployment because of trade-union monopoly labour supply in several industries. Beenstock and Minford have argued, for example, that unemployment can be reduced only 'if the restrictive practice of collective bargaining is replaced by competitive bargaining'.[7] There was no evidence of government moves in this direction in 1983–7.

The Thatcherite approach to trade unions has always been marked by a determination to seek industrial victories over strike action and to refuse to compromise or negotiate if such discussions are a ritualistic prelude to surrender. The government, since 1979, was absolutely committed to the breaking of trade-union power, in contrast to the weakness and humiliating defeats of the Heath period. One particularly clear example of this approach in the second term concerned the banning of trade unions at the government communications headquarters (GCHQ). Originally announced in January 1984 by Foreign Secretary Sir Geoffrey Howe, the rationale of the move was to prevent a repetition of eight occasions of disruptive industrial action since 1979, including a strike which had hindered intelligence gathering during the Soviet invasion of Afghanistan. The Foreign Secretary stated that 'on occasion, over 25% of GCHQ staff were involved and the degree of disruption could have had serious consequences for national security'.[8] Despite the predictable outcry from the opposition parties, the TUC and the GCHQ unions, the government refused to budge. The workers were offered £1,000 compensation and those who refused to accept the new non-union status threatened with transferal to other less sensitive civil service employment. Mrs Thatcher, defending the decision, told the Commons that:

The principle that members of organizations concerned with national security should not be members of national unions is a familiar one which already applies to the police and intelligence services. I believe the proposals we have made are the only ones which will fully reach the Government's objectives.[9]

Phillip Bassett noted that 'shocked, astonished, the unions were appalled that trade unionism could be forbidden so easily'.[10] By March, 1984, 90 per cent of GCHQ staff had relinquished union membership, leaving a handful of people to fight on with TUC support but without industrial action. The dissidents took their case to the courts but, finally, the Law Lords upheld the government's ban. The government's GCHQ victory was total despite the strength of opposition and resentment it aroused.

Apart from GCHQ, the government's largest clashes with trade union industrial power concerned the teachers, whose dispute, while never a full strike, dragged on without government concessions until the 1987 election, and the National Union of Mineworkers (NUM). The 1984–5 coal strike was momentous for both Thatcherism and the British left, and deserves further attention.

For Mrs Thatcher, there was the personal determination not to be humiliated by the miners as had Mr Heath in 1972 and 1974. Conservatives had long since drawn lessons, of which the Ridley Report advocating a tougher approach was the most celebrated, from the Heath experience. Initially the Conservatives' response was couched in terms of an economic battle with the NUM on traditional economic issues such as wages and conditions. But it became clear, after Arthur Scargill's election as NUM President, and his failure several times to procure a strike before the 1983 election, that any future dispute would be political rather than economic. Peter Hain, himself sympathetic to the NUM, has described the 1984–5 dispute as 'a political strike with industrial arguments laced with syndicalist rhetoric'.[11] One Parliamentary Private Secretary thought that 'Scargill would have liked it to be a Marxist–Leninist insurrection'.[12] Patrick Jenkin recalled that 'it was a battle to the death with Scargill. The stake was an insurrection but Scargill made the tactical mistake of not having a mandate'.[13]

Mr Scargill had repeatedly stated that he believed in class war, accepted extra-parliamentary action to overthrow a 'capitalist' government, and regarded the NUM strike as a launching pad and inspiration to other workers to join him in a socialist revolution.[14] As he told *New Left Review* in a celebrated 1975 interview:

> The issue is a very simple one: it is them and it is us. I will never accept that it is anything else because it is a class battle, it is a class war. While it is them and us, my position is perfectly clear: I want to take from them for us. In other words, I want to take into common ownership everything in Britain.[15]

For Mr Scargill, the 1984–5 strike was little to do with the NCB's pit closure programme *per se* — although he undoubtedly and genuinely opposed it. Rather, he saw an opportunity to challenge in a class war a government committed to an opposite philosophy from his own. Thatcherism challenged Scargillism by definition. Privatisation, rolling back the socialist aspects of the post-war consensus, reducing trade-union power, and increasing business opportunities all threatened what Mr Scargill, and the British left generally, held most dear. In that sense, Thatcherism did indeed 'cause' the 1984–5 strike. But in another sense Mr Scargill caused it by choosing March 1984 as the moment directly to confront the Thatcherite state of which Ian Macgregor's NCB was only a fraction. Given Mr Scargill's ideology, he had no option but to strike to prevent Thatcherism from spreading. And in a democracy he was entitled to do so. Equally, the government was entitled to stop him because the right to strike in Britain is balanced by the right of management – or the government in a political dispute – not to give in. A long, protracted, and bloody strike was therefore inevitable. One Cabinet minister recalled that 'Scargillism saved the government, giving it a popular cause at a difficult time. The defeat of Scargillism was very important in the long term'.[16] Another Cabinet minister thought that 'it was evident Scargill was spoiling for a fight and that if there was a strike it would be a large one. The Cabinet committee coordinated but you could not plan too far ahead. We dealt with the deployment of the police, took legal advice and coordinated between ministers. We could not just sit back and let Ian Macgregor get on with it'.[17]

The issue of pit closures was tailormade for both sides. For Mr Scargill, it indicated his warnings of a butchery of the industry and loss of jobs and for the NCB it represented the right to manage and place the industry on an economic, profitable basis. The decision to close Cortonwood colliery on 1 March 1984 was the culmination of the process of confrontation. As Michael Crick has argued 'the time bomb had finally gone off. On its own, the proposed closure of Cortonwood might not have led to a national strike. But Cortonwood was an example of what was happening in the industry generally'.[18] Peter Walker thought that, 'Scargill desperately wanted industrial action. It wasn't about pit closures because he wouldn't negotiate on that. His purpose was political and he went around saying that'.[19] Ian Macgregor also saw the dispute in terms of inevitability, as he explained in his memoirs:

> It had been clear from Christmas, if not before, that as soon as we tabled our plans for 1984–5 as required at the next industry consultative council, there would be an immediate reaction. I was not there to delay, or to ask the union when it was they would most like to have their strike. If, as seemed certain, Arthur Scargill was spoiling to get a strike as soon as we announced our plans, I decided there was no point in holding back – even if it might postpone the inevitable for a while. By

March we had decided on what we had to do in the year ahead. If Scargill's only reaction to the announcement of our plans was to go for a confrontation, then, in the absence of any evidence that there was a willingness on his part to negotiate, I decided we would have to place those plans firmly on the table. If we were to be faced with strike action then so be it.[20]

It is not the purpose of this account to give a blow by blow chronology of the strike,[21] but to explain why, after a 359-day strike, Thatcherism emerged clearly triumphant. A number of factors proved important to the outcome. Firstly, the political will of the government to endure such a long strike and to reject the calls for compromise was a precondition for industrial victory. Mrs Thatcher's own personal resolve in this matter, not least the chairing of a Cabinet committee to monitor the dispute, was vital. She was disinclined to make optimistic statements during the strike – light at the end of the tunnel was not discerned. In both March and April 1984 she saw no sign of an early settlement and refused to intervene with the Coal Board's management. Asked in June how long the strike would last, she replied that 'I couldn't dream of saying. I just don't know. I do not see an immediate end'.[22] By September, she stated that the government was prepared to contemplate the strike lasting for a year or more, admitting that 'we can carry on for a very, very long time – and shall . . . It does not matter how long the strike goes on – uneconomic pits have always had to be closed . . . and must always be closed. If mob violence triumphs, it is the end of democracy'.[23] Energy Secretary, Peter Walker, recalled that 'there was never a moment when there was disunity in government'.[24]

Arguably Mrs Thatcher's own personal line toughened as the strike continued. Probably her most forthright analysis was provided on the debate on the Queen's Speech in November 1984, in which she stated that:

If the leadership of the NUM, without consulting their membership, rejecting their desire for a ballot, persist in refusing this deal, the House is entitled to ask: Do they want to end this strike or do they seek to prolong it for reasons which have little to do with jobs and pay, but everything to do with extra-parliamentary challenge to this House and this Government?

Why had they chosen to seek the assistance of the Libyan government, which used its embassy for murder on the streets of London? Mr. Kinnock had been right to condemn this sinister alliance. There is no reason why this strike should go on one day longer. For the sake of the mining industry and communities, and for the sake of every miner and his family, I say: End it now. The strike was in the name of jobs but it was, in fact, destroying jobs. When customers could not rely on a secure supply of coal, they turned to other fuels. The Labour Party had supported the strike, no matter what the cost or what the damage, and no matter how many jobs were lost.[25]

Other ministers also expressed a refusal to compromise. Home Secretary Leon Brittan described the strike as an attack on the rule of law itself, and pledged full policing and expenditure to finance it, however long the dispute lasted. Mr Brittan recalled that:

The Cabinet committee considered the situation continually. The rule of law was threatened and I was determined Scargill should not succeed. I am proud to have been a member of the government that defended the rule of law. It was a watershed in our affairs.

I received daily reports of events and we were able to maintain the independence of police forces so that the right to go to work was upheld. Anyone seeking to prevent that was acting in a criminal way.[26]

Energy Secretary Peter Walker, although less than robust in his attitudes in the first few months, according to Mr Macgregor's memoirs,[27] refused to compromise on the key question of the management's right to manage. The government therefore displayed the political will necessary to endure a long and violent strike which had been conspicuously absent during the Heath administration. Peter Jenkins asks the question, though not with approval, 'was this Thatcherism's finest hour?'[28] Given the abject record of the Heath Government in 1972 and 1974, and given the centrality of the removal of the union veto on moves towards a market economy, Jenkins's question can be answered, by the Thatcherites at least, in the affirmative.

The second important factor in the defeat of the strike was the determination of the NCB leadership, Chairman Ian Macgregor and Deputy Chairman Jimmy Cowan, to refuse to compromise on the economic necessity of the pit-closure programme. To Macgregor, Mr Scargill and his supporters were 'the enemies within', as he entitled his memoirs. It was clear that sections of the NCB management did not support Mr Macgregor's tough line, which they considered over-pugnacious and likely to sour relations in the industry. Ian Macgregor considered that Ned Smith, in industrial relations, was appalled at the confrontational style, and Geoff Kirk bitterly objected to the downgrading of his PR department by the use of outsiders such as David Hart and Tim Bell. As Macgregor put it in relation to the national newspaper advertisements prepared by Tim Bell:

At one stage Tim was having advertisements drawn up and I would then take them to Geoff Kirk, telling him that they were ideas of mine, and ask him to get the Board's agency to put them out. He must have marvelled at how I became such a brilliant copywriter overnight. Throughout the summer Tim reported directly to me, but as the role of public relations became more central to the conduct of the dispute in the autumn, so he was unwillingly brought more and more into conflict with Geoff Kirk. I am sure Geoff was a staunch Labour supporter and therefore found it especially difficult to accept that Tim was paid by us as an advisor, and was limited in his activities to just that. I am sure he was convinced, quite wrongly, that the Tories, and particularly Downing Street, were now running the show.[29]

Ian Macgregor found himself in conflict not only with Mr Scargill, but with Peter Walker, whose instinct for consensus he considered unreliable in such a dispute, and with a large section of NCB senior management at its Hobart House Headquarters. This aspect of the dispute is still somewhat shrouded in mystery. Peter Walker has repudiated the Macgregor accusation and the recollection of other close participants in the handling of the strike is at variance. One senior Cabinet minister recalled that 'I was one of the pessimists. I thought it could not be an affair of only few weeks. Peter Walker told us every week that the trickle would become a flood. Peter was not defeatist but he was something a bit inclined to look for a compromise as opposed to a total victory'.[30]

Another member of the Cabinet committee considered that 'There were moments of friction. I would not agree with Macgregor or Walker. It was not a matter of hawk and dove but of how to handle the situation'.[31] Conservative Party opinion across the wet–dry spectrum was generally satisfied with Mr Walker's attitude. George Gardiner, on the right of the party, said, 'I can't remember any wet argument that we should compromise with Scargill. Peter Walker at Energy was not backsliding'.[32]

At all events, Macgregor and Walker found it difficult to establish a personal rapport. Indeed, communication was a problem for Mr Macgregor throughout the dispute. His own media performances were so uninspiring, as he admits, that Michael Eaton was drafted in as Coal Board spokesman, causing immediate confusion as to who actually was in charge on the NCB side. In order to sustain the dispute, Macgregor, Cowan and trusted outsiders such as Bell and Hart had to possess the same political will as government ministers. Ian Macgregor's own account of the dispute shows that, for him, the political aspect quickly overtook and dominated the strictly economic question of pit closures. Thus he concludes his memoirs:

> During the strike, we came within a whisper of concluding, as a nation, that the thug and the bully were immune from the law because what they were doing was sanctioned by orders from a union. We fought it and we won. Many people would say that the price was too high. But to my mind, that is the price you have to pay for freedom. The enemies of democracy are everywhere. If we are not to sink into soulless collectivism, we must realize that we cannot rely on our freedoms always being there. We cannot assume that Scargill, or any other of his like-minded pals on the left, will not make strenuous efforts again to reduce us to the state of serfdom he tried to impose on the miners as a whole. The lesson, above all lessons, to be learned from the strike, is that we cannot depend on democracy. It depends on us.[33]

Turning to the mechanics of the strike, the third important factor in ensuring a victory for Thatcherism was the availability of coal stocks. This enabled the government to promise with confidence that, even if there was a severe winter, electric power would be

maintained. Moreover, Mr Scargill's misjudgement of the extent
of coal stocks, deliberately built up for such an occurrence as the
Ridley plan had suggested, demonstrated that the situation was
different from the quick 1972 and 1974 miners' victories. As one
account of the strike has argued, the building up of 55 million
tonnes of coal stocks was government policy during the whole
Thatcher administration although during Nigel Lawson's tenure as
Energy Secretary, the policy was sharply stepped up.[34] Similarly,
the utilisation of oil-fired and nuclear generating capacity to
preserve coal stocks was undertaken. Thus 'four record surges of
demand in January 1985 failed to produce a single flicker of the
nation's lights, and General Winter, whose prospective aid had
buoyed up the miners for ten miserable months, turned out to be a
broken reed'.[35]

Fourthly, the contribution of working miners, primarily in
Nottinghamshire, assisted the government and NCB. Denied a
ballot, and shocked by intimidation from flying pickets from
Yorkshire, the Nottinghamshire miners made a significant contribution to the defeat of the NUM which, in turn, paved the way
for the foundation of the breakaway Union of Democratic Mineworkers (UDM). The coal from the 25 working Nottinghamshire
pits helped to maintain power supplies and the Trent Valley
power stations at Cottam, West Burton, and Ratcliffe-on-Soar
operated as normal. But the refusal of Nottinghamshire to strike
robbed Mr Scargill of solidarity and, once individual miners began
legal proceedings in the courts, helped to divert NUM attention to
peripheral matters rather than to the industrial battle itself.
Ultimately sequestration of NUM funds was the logical conclusion
of such legal challenges, which weakened, though not fatally, the
NUM's position. By November 1984 sequestrators, embarked on
the recovery of a £200,000 fine on the NUM, traced £2.7 million to
a Dublin bank. An Irish judge froze the money and thus frustrated
the NUM's policy of transferring funds out of Britain. Coming
only one month after the NUM's financial link with Libya was
disclosed, Mr Scargill's inability to maximise the financing of the
strike was a contributory factor in his ultimate defeat.

A fifth factor worth mentioning was the willingness of other
workers either to break the strike by crossing picket lines or to
refuse to assist the NUM. The steel workers showed little
sympathy for joining the action as the siege of Orgreave, which

supplied the Scunthorpe steel works, demonstrated. Similarly, as Norman Tebbit recalled, 'the decision of the workers at Ravenscraig to continue working was very important'.[36] Many individual railwaymen drove trains which moved coal contrary to union leaders' instructions. Lorry drivers, particularly the men employed by small independent firms, were happy to move coal by road, despite the ferocity of picketing. The appeals of T & GWU leaders not to cross picket lines were ignored. Nicholas Ridley thought that 'it did not surprise me that the lorry drivers continued working. Why shouldn't they?'.[37] Moreover, the TUC collectively offered moral support to the NUM but was unwilling to mobilise for industrial action. In any case, individual trade unionists may well have rejected calls for any political sympathy strikes. Trade-union leaders, with the exception of Eric Hammond of the EETPU and others who thought like him, offered Mr Scargill full support but were perplexed why the rank and file failed to share the same enthusiasm. The TUC leaders ended by seeking a negotiated compromise settlement – the very option that could not be available. Repelled by a Thatcherite victory over a hitherto strong union, yet disturbed by Mr Scargill's Libya links and picket line violence, the TUC vainly sought a middle way of compromise, oblivious that the corporate state world of beer and sandwiches deals had disappeared. The TUC seven, Norman Willis, David Basnett, Ray Buckton, Moss Evans, Bill Keys, Jack Eccles and Gerry Russell, sought a settlement with Peter Walker that was little more than a pedantic redefinition of words aimed at satisfying each side so that honour was intact. Although well-intentioned, the TUC's intervention to try to resolve the dispute displayed its impotence and irrelevance. One junior minister summed up the situation by recognising that 'Mrs Thatcher was able to hammer the unions in a way that we didn't foresee in 1979–80. We didn't expect the power of the unions to collapse like a pack of cards and the defeat of Scargill was the last firework'.[38] Thus, neither individually nor collectively could the trade unions rescue Mr Scargill from political defeat.

Sixthly, and finally, the use of the police to prevent picketing likely to intimidate working miners was vital to the outcome of the dispute. Arthur Scargill had claimed, with some justification, to have invented the flying pickets, whose greatest success had been the Saltley Gate closure during the 1972 miners' strike which had led directly to the Cabinet's climbdown. In 1984–5, flying pickets were countered with 'flying policemen' who enabled pits to stay open and production to continue in a way that had not occurred in 1972 and 1974. This aspect of policing was the sharp end of the policy of seeking an industrial victory. Without the use of a mobile, nationally organised police force in this way, Nottinghamshire would have come to a standstill, Orgreave would have closed, and the back to work movement would have been stillborn. The use of police in very large numbers, the arrest of pickets on the way to pits and the utilisation of horses were all features of the defeat of the flying pickets. One account of the Orgreave picketing illustrated the effect:

> When the thirty-five-vehicle convoy finally arrived, with its endless chain of police escorts, there was still one more brief moment when it looked as though Scargill's strategy might actually work. The ten-deep wall of blue uniforms broke at one point under the sheer weight of the picket-line scrum, and a few miners spilled through. They were too bemused and incredulous, though, to consolidate their advantage, and they were all quickly arrested. The breach was soon repaired with reinforcements, ambulancemen patched up face wounds and badly cut heads on both sides, and a steady stream of victims were dispatched to hospital in Rotherham.
>
> The horses went into action again, stopping the pickets from reaching Orgreave's perimeter fence, and then, as so often happened on such occasions, the disturbance died down as fast as it had originally flared. Many miners, shocked at what they had seen, just went home, and when the lorries, now loaded to the limit with coke, reappeared ninety minutes later, there was just a giant chorus of 'scab' and no further resistance. The afternoon run, after some heavy lunchtime drinking, produced a renewed storm of bottles and half-bricks, but this was largely unfocused aggression. It took only two minutes for the horses to clear the lane and put the pickets to flight.[39]

Primarily for the six reasons outlined above, Thatcherism defeated Scargillism in the 1984–5 battle. One junior minister recalled that 'it was the return match and Scargill lost. It was crucial in the eyes of overseas investors who realised that once Scargill was defeated, they could invest in Britain'.[40] For both sides it was a battle that had to be fought and the language of industrial victory necessitated a long dispute. For many in the political centre – Liberal, most Social Democrats, the Labour right and the Conservative left – it was a futile and costly dispute with few redeeming features. The post-war consensus, which had preached compromise to settle strikes and restore social harmony, was in this sense a loser in the 1984 miners' strike. Not surprisingly, those who thought only in terms of a compromise settlement appeared to be beached on a sandbank as the political tide receded from them. Thatcherism was aimed not only against Scargillism but against that post-war industrial relations consensus of which Mr Wilson and Mr Heath were the epitome. The outcome of the strike showed that for Thatcherism there was no going back on the quest for a fully operational private enterprise economy, free from any trade union, or corporate state, veto. Strangely, however, the government did not seek to make immediate political capital out of the defeat of Scargillism. Conservative MPs who were considered to be 'gloating' were discouraged. The political momentum the government had gathered was lost. Mrs Thatcher apparently did not favour rubbing in the victory. One Cabinet minister recalled that 'No. 10 said there was to be no crowing in victory. It came straight from the PM at the Cabinet meeting. People are gentle hearted and felt that the violence had gone on too long – in victory, magnaminity'.[41] Another, more senior, colleague regretted the missed opportunity: 'it was the death of the myth that the miners could bring down the government and that you could not govern without the consent of the trade-union leaders. We should have had a bloody good gloat. But No. 10 said 'No Gloating'. I don't know why because that is un-Thatcherite. But we did not achieve the *political* gain we should have'.[42] Leon Brittan, who played a crucially important role in the dispute as Home Secretary, thought that 'it was one of the great events of the 20th century and I was surprised how quickly people put it behind them, but any effort to rub it in would have been misguided'.[43] Similarly, a Treasury minister recalled that 'there was no desire to go in for a public display of gloating on any one's part. But we were disappointed that a critically important victory over the forces of subversion seemed not to be recognised by the country'.[44] One backbench Thatcherite considered that 'the miners' strike demonstrated beyond doubt the determination of the Prime Minister. Anyone who had experienced her leadership could not have thought she would give in to Scargill. Even if the miners had been united and Nottingham not working, there would still have been security of supply. I think we could have been forgiven what Norman Tebbit called after the 1987 election a 'little gloat'.[45]

Wider changes, however, have resulted from the defeat of trade-union power. The Trade-union movement is now split into those who reject Thatcherism in all its manifestations, and those who advocate a new unionism of strike-free agreements, private health care, co-operation with management, and industry-wide, rather than craft, unionism.

On the left, led by Arthur Scargill of the NUM and Rodney Bickerstaffe of the National Union of Public Employees, is a total rejection of everything Mrs Thatcher has achieved – a market-oriented economy, privatisation, and trade-union legislation. This view is supported by a number of academic industrial relations specialists such as MacInnes who repudiates the view that the industrial relations climate is improved since 1979.[46] But on the right of the union movement the 'new unionism' has emerged. Led vigorously by Eric Hammond of the Electricians' Union (EETPU) and supported by Gavin Laird's Engineering Union (AEUW) and John Lyon's power workers (EMA), the 'new unionism' has embraced the free-enterprise, entrepreneurial economy, backed privatisation and increased corporate profitability and consequently shared in the rising living standards of the Thatcher years for those in work. The 'new unionism' is, however, much more than just a political change of attitudes, important though that has been. It has sought gradually to improve industrial relations with private-sector employers by concluding no-strike agreements, moving towards single-industry unionism and promoting democratic internal union reforms based on regular balloting of the membership by the leaders.

No-strike agreements, for example, have revolutionised the industrial relations climate in a number of industries and are in marked contrast to the 'British disease' of the 1960s and 1970s, when strike action was almost a first resort. Eric Hammond's EETPU pioneered the no-strike agreement with conspicuous mutual advantages to both unions and management. The first arrangement was made in 1981 with Japanese-owned television manufacturers Toshiba at their Plymouth factory. Six of the seven unions at the plant disappeared; new ways of working were introduced; demarcation disputes were eliminated; full employee consultation in decision making; disputes resolved by binding arbitration; and no strikes. Six years on and Toshiba workers are more than satisfied with the outcome, with wages rising steadily and an employee dividend scheme introduced in 1983 whereby if bottom line profits rise above a certain agreed level, 75 per cent of the extra profit goes into the dividend. In its first years of operation, all employees benefited by receiving an extra £200 in this way.[47]

In other firms strike-free agreements have also succeeded. At Sanyo (UK), employees are expected to work in any job which they are capable of doing. In-plant training is provided and job rotation is practised throughout the company. There are no job descriptions and all production, inspection and most clerical staff are paid the same salary. Not only Japanese-owned companies such as Sanyo, Toshiba, and most recently Nissan in North East England have embraced the no-strike agreements. At Inmos, dealing in micro-electronics, unions and management agree to 'respond flexibly and quickly to changes in the pattern of demand for the company's products and to technological innovation'. Similarly at A. B. Electronics, both sides have agreed to 'the maximum co-operation and support from all employees in achieving a completely flexible, well-motivated workforce, capable of transferring on a temporary or permanent basis to work of any nature that is within the capabilities of such employees, having such regard to the provisions of adequate training and safety arrangements'.[48]

Left-wing trade-union leaders have bitterly criticised such agreements pioneered by EETPU. Tom Sawyer, NUPE's deputy general secretary, has commented that 'if no-strike deals continue then trade unions become part of the management'. Ken Gill, Britain's most senior communist union leader, thinks that 'the difference between a slave and a worker is the right to withdraw his labour . . . [the new unionism] . . . denies workers the ultimate expression of rejection'.[49] Such views, while often vociferously expressed, have made no headway in restricting the growth of no-strike agreements. Equally as important has been the growth of single-industry unionism which has replaced the chaotic craft

union system where up to twenty or so different unions could be
represented in one industry – each competing against the other in
demarcation disputes and by 'leapfrogging' wage claims. The 'new
unionism' has swept away such backwardness. All the EETPU's
and many other union's new arrangements are single-union. Fewer
and fewer employers are now prepared to sign deals with more
than one union, thus removing duplication, hassle and the
potentiality for inter-union strife. James MacFarlane of the
Engineering Employers' Federation has agreed that 'the single
union agreement must surely become the logical norm and not just
where they are set up by foreign owners or away from traditional
industrial centres'.[50] Finally, the centrality of ballots and consultation is a marked feature of the 'new unionism'. Workers who own
shares in industry now outnumber trade unionists for the first time;
many unionists own shares in privatised industries; 67 per cent of
households are owner-occupiers; and credit cards and consumer
borrowing are not just for the salaried professional classes. All
these factors make it less likely that workers regularly balloted by
their unions will wish to resort to damaging strike action. The new
unionism is rooted in the democratic support of individuals who
are unlikely to be impressed either by the Labour Party's hostility
to Mrs Thatcher's reforms or Arthur Scargill's calls for increased
revolutionary consciousness to overthrow capitalism. In Mrs
Thatcher's privatised, entrepreneurial economy the 'new unionism' may have a future more promising than that offered by
traditionally militant unionism.

CHAPTER 4

The Scope of Thatcherism and Privatisation

Privatisation, or denationalisation as it was once called, has been central to Thatcherism. The rolling back of the Socialist state and encouragement of the free-market are encapsulated in the privatisation programme. The increased size of the private sector in relation to the public sector seemed a distant dream for most Conservatives before 1979 – according to the socialist ratchet argument of Sir Keith Joseph[1] – and therefore the extent of privatisation, according to Thatcherite ideology, has been a triumph. No less than 40 per cent of the industries nationalised in 1945–79 have been privatised. At the same time, bus and coach routes have been de-regulated, contracting out to private tender has become a feature of Conservative-run local government, private pensions, health care and education have flourished and professional restrictive practices, such as the solicitors' conveyancing monopoly, have been eroded. Six freeports have been established and enterprise zones expanded. Over 1 million council houses have been sold to tenants. This process, as John Biffen has remarked with some irony, is a permanent and fundamental transfer of wealth and power in favour of the private sector. Individual share owners stood at 2 million in 1979 and had subsequently grown to 9.2 million by 1987, for the first time outnumbering trade unionists, many of whom had bought shares in privatised companies. Nigel Lawson predicted that as a result a 'new army of shareholders would prevent the Labour party putting the genie of individual ownership and participation back into the nationalised bottle'.[2] Backbench dry, George Gardiner, considered that 'before 1983, we did not cotton on to the possibilities of popular share floatation. It did not lend itself to dispute between wets and dries and everyone jumped on the bandwagon'.[3] In both economic and political terms, the effects of the privatisation programme have been radical. Economically, the corporate power of the nationalised sector has been broken and discredited by the financial health of privatised companies. And politically, the process has yielded considerable electoral dividends for the Conservative Party. Thus one junior minister thought that 'the political

TABLE 4.1   Privatisations 1979–87

Enterprise	Date begun	Proceeds (£)
British Petroleum	1979	827
National Enterprise Board Holdings	1979	294
British Aerospace	1981	389
North Sea Licences	1981	349
British Sugar Corporation	1981	44
Cables and Wireless	1981	1 024
Amersham International	1982	64
National Freight Consortium	1982	5
Britoil	1982	1 053
Associated British Ports	1983	97
International Aeradio	1983	60
British Rail Hotels	1983	45
Jaguar	1984	297
Sealink	1984	66
Wytch Farm	1984	82
British Telecom	1984	3 682
BT Loan Stock	1984	158
Enterprise Oil	1984	382
British Shipbuilders Warship Yards	1985	54
British Gas (one-third paid)	1986	5 090
British Airways Helicopters	1986	13
British Gas debt	1986	750
BT preference shares	1986	250
TSB	1986	800
Unipart 1987	1987	52
Leyland Bus	1987	4
Leyland Trucks	1987	0
British Airways (half paid)	1987	825
Royal Ordnance	1987	190
Rolls-Royce (half paid)	1987	1 360
Miscellaneous	1979–87	510
Total		18 816

advent of privatisation was a clear way of influencing the electorate – it was a sensible and popular policy. The British have always
been followers of horse-racing who like to put a few shillings on a
winner – privatisation was putting a few bob on a sure winner'.[4]
Moreover as Table 4.1 indicates, the Exchequer has raised more
than £18 billion.

Although the pace of privatisation accelerated after 1983, the
method of doing so was established in the first term. There was no
attempt to liquidate chronic loss-making nationalised industries to
permit private sector re-structuring as would occur with any
bankrupt firm. Some advocates of privatisation favoured this course.
The Times in an editorial argued with sound economic logic that:

> If unsuccessful businesses were transferred to private hands at
> nominal prices and their new managers restored them to health,
> the ultimate result would be much better for society than if they
> were to stay in government ownership and lose money indefi-
> nitely. The unprofitability of a nationalised industry does not
> alone justify the deferment of privatisation. The case for priva-
> tising competitive industries is, therefore, the same as the case
> for competition. When a competitive industry is artificially
> contained in one enterprise and that enterprise is publicly
> owned, managers lack the discipline imposed by shareholders.
> As they believe that the state will, in the final analysis, cover
> their losses, there is a temptation to enjoy a quiet life by
> maintaining too many unprofitable operations. The perpetua-
> tion of unprofitable operations is evidence of resource mis-
> allocation and economic inefficiency.[5]

Instead, loss-makers would be set break-even targets followed
by profit targets prior to floatation. That private sector competitive atmosphere was to be simulated in order to prepare for
privatisation. Loss-makers such as Rolls-Royce and British Airways were privatised most successfully this way; but the process is
a slower one for industries such as coal, steel, railways and
shipbuilding. Considerable subsidisation has been required before
break-even targets are in sight and while the days of uncontrolled
losses are over, such industries are still loss-makers nonetheless.

For profitable industries such as British Telecom and British
Gas privatisation has been a much swifter process, yielding

considerable government revenue as a by-product. Problems, however, have arisen with the transfer of public monopolies to private monopolies with little improvement in customer satisfaction beyond greater price stability. British Telecom, following privatisation, held prices steady for three years, for example. Other accounts have already described the privatisation process.[6] This account aims to explain why the government privatised certain industries but was unable to privatise others, and what consequences flowed therefrom.

Shortly after the 1983 General Election, it was evident that the government wished to step up the privatisation process with the Treasury pushing for the most radical solution. Outside government, other voices urged radicalism. The Institute of Economic Affairs preferred wholesale privatisation and Michael Beesley and Stephen Littlechild, writing in the July 1983 *Lloyds Bank Review*, advocated a privatisation process embracing 80 per cent of nationalised industries including the NCB, British Rail, Electricity and the Post Office. (Ironically none had been privatised by 1988.) Within government, hints of a similarly bold approach began to emerge. In November 1983 John Moore, Financial Secretary to the Treasury, stated that 'as the programme moves into the heartlands of the public sector, maximising competition will become of dominant importance. No state monopoly is sacrosanct. We intend through competition and privatisation, to open up the state sector to the stimulus of competition and reverse the creeping bureaucratization of the last thirty five years'.[7]

Subsequently, it transpired that the Treasury preferred an all-embracing nationalised industry Act, allowing ministers to hire and fire state industry Chairmen and board members, to order capital re-structuring and remodel the financial targets. More significantly, however, ministers would be able to order *ad hoc* privatisation of viable sectors of overall loss-makers. The Treasury paper advocated that 'all industries would be given the power to set up subsidiaries under the Companies Acts and transfer property, rights and liabilities to them. This restructuring may or may not be a prelude to privatisation. Powers, involving a parliamentary procedure, would also be taken allowing ministers to require that assets and activities are privatised in accordance with their instructions'.[8]

The plan did not reach fruition. By November 1985 the Treasury proposals had been abandoned in favour of the existing industry-by-industry privatisation programme. Nationalised industry chairmen, primarily Sir Denis Rooke of British Gas, lobbied successfully against the scheme in private, and legislative plans were scuppered. But outside interest in such a scheme has continued. Kevin Dowd has proposed 'an omnibus bill to get rid of all the nationalised industries at one go. The Act would simply order the Government to divest itself of all its commercial assets within a stated period . . . the shares being given equally to everyone in the country who would have the right to do exactly what they wanted with them'.[9]

Radicalism of that kind was off the agenda. Instead the government pressed ahead with orthodox privatisation. In April 1984 Sealink was targeted for privatisation, joining Jaguar in swift and successful transfers to profitability in the private sector. In Jaguar's case the transformation was exceptional. Profitability and export sales soared under John Egan's astute chairmanship and soon the company was recruiting more workers. Although many of the 'smaller' privatisations were equally as successful in economic terms, public attention concentrated on the large floatations, enabling shareholders to realise almost instant profits. While it may be argued that such a process gives investors a false impression that all shares are likely to rise irrespective of market conditions, it was undeniably the case that the widely publicised floatations of British Telecom, the Trustee Savings Bank (TSB), and British Gas caught the public mood. Privatisation became 'popular capitalism', its effects felt way beyond the City or traditional investors. Michael Heseltine considered that, in political terms, 'the three million new share owners and the 400,000 who now hold shares in the former state businesses which employ them are enjoying the fruits of a profound and wholly benign revolution in which there are no losers. . . It is indeed a fundamental shift of wealth and it has only just begun'.[10]

The British Telecom launch in December 1984, then the world's largest, was an instant success with BT employees, who eagerly accepted preferential terms, and with the public. Shares opened at a high premium of 45p over the issue price of 50p required of the 2.25 million people allocated shares. Oblivious to the popularity of BT privatisation, Mr Kinnock promised that Labour would renationalise at the price for which it was sold, thus preventing anyone making a profit. This policy dismayed shop stewards at British Telecom's factory in Mr Kinnock's constituency who asked the Labour leader if they could keep their shares. 'The question unsettled Mr. Kinnock', noted one reporter, 'especially since it indicated a mood which goes far wider than BT employees'.[11] As Finer has argued 'the point is not that the current ownership of shares is very widely dispensed but that for the first time it seems as if a way of making it popular has been discovered'.[12]

The Trustee Savings Bank sale in 1986 was similarly popular. The offer was seven times oversubscribed with £5.6 billion put up by 1.3 million priority applicants and 3.7 million public applicants. Lazard Brothers, who handled the sale, estimated that more than 1 million people receiving TSB shares were first-time shareholders. The third major privatisation aiming to extend 'popular capitalism' was the most ambitious: British Gas, which was launched, after the much criticised Sid campaign, in December 1986. The £5 billion share sale was five times oversubscribed and the rising value of the shares after the launch produced inordinate satisfaction for investors. As Peter Walker, the Energy Secretary, recalled, 'Gas privatisation was very popular. When NALGO organised rallies against it, only 6 people or so turned up and 99% of Gas workers bought shares'.[13]

The British Gas sale, however, attracted similar criticism to that of BT in that a public monopoly was being transformed into a private one with little advantage to the consumer. In terms of the ultimate Thatcherite aim of promoting a competitive, free-enterprise economy, this criticism is valid. As one study had predicted 'privatisation in its present form will at best provide only weak incentives for improved efficiency. There will be no change in the incentives provided by competition in the product market'.[14] Some critics have gone further. Thompson has stated that 'it is not clear what overall benefits will be generated by the change in *ownership* of the nationalised industries' (emphasis in original).[15] The obvious reply is that the change of ownership has in many cases liberated the taxpayer from perpetually subsidising industries which had precious little incentive to run themselves even moderately efficiently. While greater competition would have been desirable in cases such as BT and British Gas, the change in ownership was especially worthwhile in former loss-makers; for example Rolls-Royce, BA and Jaguar. Private ownership, by definition, has removed the prop of potential state subsidy to bail out the consequence of either slothful management or trade-union restrictive practices. John Moore has thus argued that 'if the Government stands behind nationalised industries ... with a bottomless purse, it is no wonder that inefficiencies flourish and market responsiveness does not stand very high in an industry's scale of priorities'.[16]

However, it must be borne in mind that privatisation in the British context would be a more lengthy process if greater competition was the sole criterion for action. Fewer industries could have been privatised in 1983–7 had the government broken up BT and British Gas as a condition of privatisation. The justification for the government's policy was not economic but strictly political. As long as the Labour Party threatened renationalisation or social ownership, as it did up to and beyond the 1987 Election, the political situation required the government to maximise the number of privatisations to forestall any future Labour administration. Thus a Labour Government, faced with a large number of privatisations, would have to renationalise them all first before extending the process to those industries which had always been in the private sector. The Thatcher Government's policy was therefore an insurance policy against this prospect. In fact, although Labour strongly opposed each privatisation and threatened renationalisation at the time, it had transpired by 1987 that Mr Kinnock and the Shadow Cabinet were giving greater stress to a Keynesian economic strategy than to formal nationalisation. Whether this stance survives, prospers or is jettisoned by Labour in future years is still open to conjecture. But the fact remains that while Labour envisages and stresses nationalisation of any kind – unlike its counterparts in Spain, Portugal, Australia, New Zealand and France – the Conservatives will have a strong incentive to privatise in haste. Thus, in turn, as Veljanovski has concluded 'the desire to proceed with the sales as fast as possible necessitated a bargain with [nationalised industry] management – agreement to support privatisation in return for the retention of the utility intact and interim restrictions on the degree of competition'.[17] Competition is consequently sacrificed at this stage of privatisation and deferred to a future stage when the threat of public ownership may have been removed.

One feature of privatisation that became apparent in the 1983–7 period was the problematic and uncertain nature of the timing of individual floatations. Plans to privatise the Water Boards, boosting revenue by £5 billion, were announced in March 1986 but dropped in July. The industry's management had been hostile in many cases (but not all) and Len Hill, Chairman of the Water Authorities' Association, criticised the rush to privatise without a longer consultation period on how this was to be done. However, what finally convinced the Cabinet to delay was the reluctance to proceed with a contentious privatisation with an election so close. Mrs Thatcher felt the need for a light legislative session with all proposed Bills becoming law by mid-1987, in order to maximise options for general election timing. Water privatisation was consequently postponed despite the disappointment this aroused among Conservative MPs, particularly as Environment Secretary, Nicholas Ridley had been regarded as an arch-privatiser.

The British Airways privatisation developed on quite different lines. Originally, there was scepticism that its sale would be practicable but in the end it was successfully removed from the public sector before the 1987 Election. In August 1983 Sir John King, BA's Chairman, indicated that privatisation would occur a year ahead of schedule in 1985, especially as profitability was climbing impressively. A £544 million loss in 1981–2 was transformed into a £77 million profit in just one year and staff overmanning eliminated by shedding 21,000 posts. Even *Concorde* was moving into profitability after years of sustaining heavy losses. In December 1983, Nicholas Ridley was able to tell the Commons that:

> Following this transformation of British Airways' financial prospects, I have decided to aim for privatisation as soon as possible, hopefully in early 1985. To this end, I propose to establish British Airways as a public limited company under Government ownership in accordance with the 1980 Act. I am accordingly arranging for the registration of a public limited company under the name of British Airways PLC, without at this stage giving it the right to trade, and I shall shortly make an order nominating it as the successor company to the British Airways Board under section 3(2) of the 1980 Act. British Airways has remained for too long preparing for take-off. It is a

great tribute to Lord King, the British Airways Board and the entire staff of the airline that I can today position the airline on the runway for take-off into the private sector.[18]

External circumstance then intervened to delay the privatisation process. BA became involved in a dispute with BCal over the CAA's award of a licence to fly the London to Riyadh route. BCal further postulated that BA's route network should be broken up, fearing that a privatised BA would exhibit monopolistic tendencies, forcing the smaller independents out of business. Some smaller companies in turn feared the predatory potential of BCal in taking over profitable routes. The industry was locked in dispute. Secondly, legal action in the American courts following the collapse of Laker Airways added considerable delay. Agreement between Britain and the United States over disputed airline capacity on transatlantic routes was more difficult to achieve than expected, materialising only in September 1986. A management buy-out plan orchestrated by Lord King was rejected by Mrs Thatcher in March 1986 because the government preferred that BA should be sold to as wide a cross-section of shareholders as possible.

It was not until October 1986 that John Moore, the Transport Secretary, was able to announce privatisation for early 1987. Lord King commented that 'this is very welcome news ... the Government's confidence is a just reward to everyone at BA whose efforts have contributed to the remarkable change in the Company's fortunes in recent years'.[19] Along with the 1987 British Airports' privatisation, the BA sale represented a classic case of how successfully privatisation operated under the Thatcher Government.

With the exception of Jaguar, the component parts of the BL empire demonstrated the limits to privatisation caused by *ad hoc* difficulties and political opposition from certain sections of the Conservative Party. The Thatcher Government was aware that it had generously subsidised BL since 1979 and the Prime Minister was impatient at its continuing problems. Michael Edwardes has described Mrs Thatcher's first meeting with his board in 1979 as somewhat typical – 'well, Mr. Edwardes, why should we pour further funds into British Leyland? She glared stonily around the table at each of us in turn'.[20] By 1986, Mrs Thatcher's attitude was basically similar. Referring to the £3.8 billion BL had received since nationalisation she stated that 'This cannot continue. We are concerned that British Leyland should be competitive. The talks going on are to achieve the future of a strong British Leyland'.[21] But one Cabinet minister recalled that 'B.L. was difficult because the view from No. 10 was that it was a plague and that it would eventually have to be closed down'.[22]

The talks were with Ford and General Motors who had both expressed interest in purchasing parts of BL. Ford envisaged a merger with BL and the government favoured this approach as a way of discharging BL from the public sector. But a backbench rebellion led by Mr Heath showed that Conservative MPs were frightened of possible job losses in marginal constituencies – the same argument used to justify further subsidy since 1974. Some opponents of the sale professed a patriotic desire to see BL remain British, oblivious to the fact that customers at home and overseas buy for quality, not for such sentimental reasons. To listen to some Conservative MPs from the Midlands was to get the impression that BL was a world-respected market leader rather than an unsuccessful loss-making nationalised concern. But the rebellion was effective, forcing Cabinet to overrule Mrs Thatcher and Nigel Lawson, and to veto Ford's acquisition. In the wake of the Westland Affair, sound economic judgement was sacrificed to a grubby political reality. One backbench Thatcherite bemoaned that 'I was angry with the West Midlands MPs. Coming after Westland, it was essential that we all close ranks and support the government'.[23] And a junior minister thought that 'my inclination was to sell BL to Ford but the West Midlands MPs just wouldn't have it. The commercial judgment was overturned by political considerations and the post-Westland effect on the Midlands marginals'.[24]

A similar fate befell the General Motors interest in Land Rover and BL's truck division. Again, all the Thatcherite arguments suggested that the sale would make sense. Public money would no longer be put at risk. Re-structuring would lead to greater financial viability which, if successful in the long run, would provide more jobs – as had occurred at Jaguar. But the 'patriotic' arguments were again the cause of backbench disquiet, whipped up also by the Labour Party's support for 'British' as opposed to

'American' industry. The government was forced to insist on retaining a 51 per cent controlling stake in Land Rover which General Motors could not accept for sound commercial reasons. The talks collapsed as ministers were warned that 50 Conservative MPs would rebel if GM's takeover was successful. GM executives blamed the breakdown of negotiations on the government's decision to bow to backbench pressure. By then, as one commentator asserted, 'the size of Mrs Thatcher's majority became one of the brakes on radical Thatcherism'.[25]

This view was confirmed by a Cabinet minister close to the issue who lamented that 'The Chief Whip told me that Land Rover would not get through. The [backbench] rebels were wrong about the industrial logic. There wouldn't have been the loss of jobs in the West Midlands that they feared'.[26] With reluctance, and with her hand forced, Mrs Thatcher insisted that GM's stake should be limited to 49 per cent and that voting control should remain with British institutions holding the other 51 per cent. GM wanted control, but would have accepted the appointment of an independent supervisory board, charged with ensuring that GM met assurances on continued production and employment. After the talks were over, GM simply commented that it was unfortunate that their proposal had not been accepted. Nor was a management buy-out plan more successful as the unhappy BL saga continued to dog yet another administration. One critic of the continued public sector status of BL went as far as to argue that 'much of the enthusiasm in some quarters for a management buy-out stems from the assumption that this Government (or a future one) is more likely to be receptive to pleas for special treatment from British owner/managers than from General Motors'.[27]

Overall, despite the problems with BL, the water board privatisation postponement and the reluctance to privatise all or part of such loss-makers as Coal, Steel and British Rail, the privatisation programme in 1983–7 demonstrated the scope rather than the limits of Thatcherism. The large number of privatisations, the increase in the private-sector vigour and profitability, and the acceptance of privatisation as a normal part of the political landscape all exemplified Thatcherism. The political dividends were also considerable with the emergence of popular capitalism further eroding Labour's voting base among the skilled working class. Few of the workers in the privatised industries are now willing, let alone positively eager, to return to nationalised control. Kavanagh has gone as far as to argue that:

> What is remarkable is how little political opposition there has been to the programme to date. In spite of complaints by leaders of trade unions, many of their members bought up the shares. There were few strikes and in Parliament, Labour's opposition was usually focused more on the 'giveaway' price at which shares were sold, rather than on the principle of privatisation. In Parliament in late 1985, the Labour deputy-leader Roy Hattersley remained silent when challenged by Nigel Lawson to state which privatised firms and industries would be renationalised, and Mr. Kinnock suggested that renationalisation would not be a high priority for a future Labour government.[28]

The method of privatisation may be subject to legitimate debate, especially when customer satisfaction requires greater competition, but few people outside the Labour Party now believe that Jaguar, Unipart, BA, Sealink, British Rail Hotels and BP would be more efficient and provide a better service to the public under nationalisation. The Alliance has softened its doubts on privatisation and Mr Steel, during the 1987 General Election campaign, speculated that the steel industry could be a privatisation target. Dr Owen's belief in the social-market economy is likely to survive the Alliance's post-election rupture, and British Social Democracy, which in Gaitskell's day opposed further nationalisation according to Clause IV, is now reconciled to extending the benefits of the market.[29] Even some members on the right of the Labour Party – Austin Mitchell, for example – have expressed doubts on the desirability, as opposed to the practicality, of further nationalisation. Judged by its own ideological convictions, privatisation has been one of the success stories of Thatcherism.

CHAPTER 5

The Scope of Thatcherism and Foreign Policy

It may be objected that, as Thatcherism is primarily an economic ideology, a distinctive Thatcherite foreign policy would be difficult to discern; that Prime Ministers sooner or later take a preponderant interest in foreign affairs, and that Mrs Thatcher is no different from her predecessors. However, what has made her approach to foreign policy unique is that she has conducted international relations in an era when the post-war consensus on British defence policy has collapsed, leaving a clear contrast between a Thatcherite pro-NATO, pro-nuclear stance and the unilateralism of the Labour Party (and sections of the Liberal Party). Moreover, her intensely nationalistic foreign policy is in clear contrast to the internationalism of all her post-war predecessors, with the possible exception of Anthony Eden at Suez. According to one backbench foreign policy specialist, 'she didn't have a foreign affairs background like all other Conservative Prime Ministers and when she arrived, she didn't have much foreign policy luggage, just patriotism and an anti-Soviet rhetoric'.[1]

Mrs Thatcher displays her patriotism by way of her foreign policy. To her immediate predecessors, patriotism was expressly edited out, as a vulgar distraction, from the more delicate arena of diplomacy. Thatcherism, therefore, has a distinct foreign policy style and content which was exemplified by the Falklands conflict in 1982. As Kavanagh states, 'in foreign affairs, Mrs. Thatcher has proved something of a "little Englander" ... She is impatient with diplomatic niceties ... but, over time, she has come to enjoy summits and gatherings of heads of state'.[2] This has become particularly the case when her international status as the senior statesman of the Western World elevated her standing with the

British public. A summit abroad is a carefully orchestrated event during a general election campaign. Nevertheless, as Riddell points out, Mrs Thatcher has a Gaullist approach 'though possibly more in leadership than policy views'[3] which gives the impression of belligerence and hectoring. These qualities may well dent her popularity at home, particularly on caring or social issues, but abroad they are welcomed as 'standing up for Britain', evoking a populist response which has been traditionally shunned by the opinion-forming foreign policy elite in Whitehall, the academic world, international think tanks and sections of the televised media. 'She just doesn't like foreigners', recalled one former foreign office minister, 'she doesn't enjoy European summits and she only enjoys visiting Washington and using anti-Soviet rhetoric'.[4]

However, the extent of Mrs Thatcher's nationalism has scarcely been muted by Britain's international commitments – member of NATO, the EEC, the Council of Europe, the OECD, one of the five permanent members of the UN Security Council, and the pivotal diplomatic force in the Commonwealth. Thatcherism in foreign policy often collides with such commitments, but is rarely blunted by them. In this sense, Thatcherism transcends the foreign policy responsibilities inherited from its predecessors in 1979. Only membership of NATO is enthusiastically embraced, while other commitments are tolerated with varying degrees of reluctance. Mrs Thatcher's irritability with the whole concept of the Commonwealth during the South African sanctions dispute of Summer 1986 was publicly evident to such an extent that it was suggested that the Queen was worried about future Commonwealth harmony. Similarly, in Autumn 1987, Mrs Thatcher displayed a veiled contempt for possible UN collaboration to patrol the Gulf,[5] preferring instead to rely on the British presence and that of other NATO allies. In the first Thatcher term, the Falklands War dominated foreign affairs, casting a lengthening shadow by way of the Fortress Falklands policy. In the second term, Thatcherism concentrated on relations with the EEC, defence policy and disarmament proposals, non-NATO Anglo–American relations, and Commonwealth pressure economically to isolate the Pretoria regime.

Mrs Thatcher has never been a fanatical supporter, in the Ted Heath, Roy Jenkins or David Steel mould, of Britain's membership of the EEC. In the early 1970s, she supported entry but without enthusiasm. However, it must be pointed out that she never seriously embraced either the arguments of the economic anti-marketeers, or the sovereignty viewpoint associated with Enoch Powell.[6] By the 1984 European Assembly elections, she was still pursuing this middle way, criticising the Labour party for being 'Europhobes' and the Alliance as 'Eurofanatics'. But since 1979, she has constantly clashed with Britain's EEC partners, transforming successive summits into acrimonious and bitter disputes. On both the issues of Britain's budget rebate and the reform of the Common Agricultural Policy (CAP), Mrs Thatcher has emerged as a *de facto* anti-marketeer. Nor does monetary union and co-operation excite her. Richard Cottrell comments that 'she has always harboured a suspicion that committing sterling to the EMS would turn the Bank of England into the local branch of the Bundesbank'.[7] Entry to the EMS has been vetoed. One former foreign office minister considered that 'she doesn't believe in Europe and took no part in the 1975 referendum. Her attitude is a reaction to Ted [Heath's] commitment'.[8]

Mrs Thatcher has been a consistent critic of the EEC for the very good Thatcherite reason that the CAP, and its funding, dominates the EEC, consuming some 70 per cent of total funds. More than that, the CAP is the world's most protectionist organisation, grossly distorting world trade to the mutual disadvantage of North and South, and provoking trade hostility within the Western world. In its operation, the CAP is run on the opposite of Thatcherite principles. Price fixing, subsidies, tariffs, surpluses, dumping, bureaucracy and consumer dissatisfaction are its hallmarks. The CAP consumes £2.5 billion per annum alone in direct subsidy, pushes food costs for the average household £13 per week higher than market prices, and erects further costs by tariffs and quotas on non-EEC produce. What began as the well-intentioned efforts to guarantee the livelihoods of the 25 per cent of the population that worked on the land in the original six EEC Countries in 1957 has grown into a gigantic monument of human waste, perversity and, when food stocks are destroyed, obscenity. As Cottrell argues, 'the CAP has wrecked the hopes for a community which might stand comparison with the superpowers'.[9]

Thus, as the EEC and the CAP have become inseparable and synonymous, so Mrs Thatcher's determination to prize their glue apart has intensified. Diana Elles notes that 'the style and tone of Mrs. Thatcher's observations are, of course, resented by the governments of the other member states... what [they] find hard to swallow is the patent honesty and clarity of Mrs. Thatcher'.[10] Thus, as Peter Jenkins has noted, in relation to her demands of budgetary rebates, 'Mrs Thatcher seemed to take positive delight in offending against the European canon. She struck a position entirely nationalistic, demanding "my" money back'.[11] Some academic proponents of the EEC have also found Mrs Thatcher's approach too abrasive. Ali M. El-Agraa believes her public display of antagonism to be unjustified – 'after all those dealing with important and sensitive issues are supposed to be both politicians and diplomats'.[12] Not only has Mrs Thatcher repeatedly attacked the EEC over the budget and the CAP but she seemed to relish the prospect. At the June 1983 summit, for example, while Gaston Thorn, the commission President, was bemoaning that 'the summit came close to breaking down' and Pierre Mauroy, the French Prime Minister described a 'very rough battle',[13] Mrs Thatcher was pleased because of Britain's rebate. It meant, she explained patiently, that over the past four years Britain had received back some £2,500 million in rebates which worked out at 65.5 per cent. This, she emphasised, was very near the two-thirds target which Britain had always sought. Since she had believed when she arrived that nobody was remotely interested in giving Britain any money at all, she said she was very satisfied with the result, however sceptical some people might be about it.

As well as further criticism of the EEC for prevaricating over the rebate, Mrs Thatcher also criticised the EEC's failure to condemn strongly enough the shooting down of the South Korean airliner by the Soviet Union in September 1983. The EEC position was 'totally inexplicable' and 'incomprehensible'. This attack was followed by continued wrangles over the budget. A contingency Bill was drafted (but not enacted) to block British budgetary contributions in the event of the breakdown of talks on the future of the CAP, prompting Gaston Thorn to accuse the British government of destroying the foundations of the EEC. The Athens summit in December 1983 was regarded as a fiasco. After three days of dispute over the budget, Mrs Thatcher was unsparing in her criticism of the 'horse trading' she said had been going on between countries who wanted to fob Britain off with yet another fudged compromise. She poured scorn on the way 'some other countries had run away from the problems'. 'All the others are takers', she said, 'and I do resent it very much when they talk about British demands. We are not making demands. We are giving notice that we cannot continue paying in as much as we pay now'.[14] It was not even possible to agree a final statement because the ten European leaders decided that anything they stated in writing could only make matters worse.

Mrs Thatcher's stance was attacked by Edward Heath, who believed that she was obsessed with the trivia of Europe. In a clear reference to the Prime Minister, Mr Heath said 'let us not get ourselves bogged down in eternal bickering about the size of Britain's net contribution, a mere fraction of 1 per cent of our national income, while letting the policies from which we stand to gain so much go by default'.[15] This view was the opposite of Mrs Thatcher's, as was demonstrated by her refusal to increase EEC funds until the case for budget reforms was met. In Rome, she informed Italian leaders that the EEC faced bankruptcy unless reform on lines suggested by Britain was forthcoming.

Again, at the March 1984 summit at Brussels, Mrs Thatcher stood alone against the existing financing and structure of CAP spending. The blocking of Britain's rebate was castigated as reprehensible and intolerable and the Prime Minister told the House of Commons that the Cabinet would consider retaliatory action. Mr Heath threatened to vote against any such move but Mrs Thatcher was warmly praised by Lord Wilson of Rievaulx and Viscount Tonypandy, for defending British interests. Although Mrs Thatcher did not press the Cabinet to withhold Britain's EEC contribution, this option gained ground within the Conservative party and remained a weapon for potential future use. One perceptive student of European affairs, John Ardargh, summed up the deadlock and ruptured relations in 1984 following the acrimonious Brussels summit. Writing from Paris, where almost twenty years before, General de Gaulle had antagonised his EEC partners, Ardargh found that:

I have found one major fear haunting Paris today. A senior French diplomat summed it up: That woman is an old-fashioned nationalist with no feeling for the European ideal. She reckons merely in terms of accountancy, not the broader political vision that is needed. Our worry is that, even with the budget solved, Britain will still drag its feet. . . Seen from Paris, the British government appears to express little belief in the need to develop the Community's institutions, its oft-repeated refusal to join the European Monetary System demonstrating that it does not want to play much part in economic integration either. Whereas all countries, France included, are wary of too much 'supranationalism', the British especially are judged to be stubbornly opposed to relinquishing any jot of sovereignty. Yet without some such moves, the Community cannot easily progress.[16]

Within months, however, progress of sorts was achieved. At Fontainebleau, it was agreed that Britain's budgetary contributions should be reduced in return for agreement to increase the Community's financial resources. Thus, as Diana Elles noted, 'Mrs. Thatcher won the major arguments on budgetary discipline and arranged a more equitable contribution to the Community's financial resources'.[17] But the raising of the VAT contribution ceiling to 1.4 per cent, although a short-term solution to the 1984 CAP expenditure problem, simply delayed an eventual solution to the CAP – total dismemberment by repatriation to the governments of member states. The CAP juggernaut picked up pace as a result of the VAT own resources re-structuring with the principles of self-sufficiency and autarky still producing vast economic misallocation of resources by ignoring supply and demand pressures as well as international comparative advantage.

Following the settlement of the budget rebate problem, attention then focused on the CAP and prospects for its fundamental reform. But all too often, Mrs Thatcher found herself in a minority of one, fighting the vested interests of European governments desperately propping up the CAP to maximise their own farming vote – a political force made more potent by the fragmented parliamentary arithmetic of countries operating proportional representation. Indeed, the French agriculture minister, Francois Guillaume, a former president of the French farmers' union, made clear his opposition to all CAP reform plans which cut subsidies, and publicly called for Britain to be expelled from the EEC. Even Michael Jopling, the agriculture minister, while not an advocate of repatriation of the CAP or free-market agriculture, was forced to concede that 'it is not in the interests of our farmers ... for the CAP to lumber on into still greater surpluses and expense until it smashes finally over the cliffs'.[18] Undaunted, M. Guillaume firmly announced, on arriving in Brussels, that the main aim of the CAP was to ensure a higher income for European farmers. He spoke out against proposed reforms of the cereals and beef sectors, including a 'co-responsibility tax' of 3 per cent on cereals, which he said would generate bureaucracy and weaken competitiveness. Such sentiments showed the impossibility of any agreed political reform of the CAP.

Not surprisingly, therefore, the group of Conservative MPs favouring an end to the CAP became increasingly more vocal. In April 1986, Mrs Thatcher had a private meeting at the Commons with ten representatives of the seventy-two strong group. The Reform Group claimed that Britain could declare its independence on agriculture without jeopardising its relationship with other Common Market countries. The MPs argued that Britain imports goods worth billions of pounds from other community members each year and our expulsion would not be in the interests of any member state. Such radical solutions, while politically impossible in 1983–7, were now forcing themselves onto the political agenda. Teddy Taylor, one of its leading proponents, recalled that 'the European Reform Group was about 70 strong with 12 activists but we did not achieve anything. Mrs Thatcher accepts the intellectual arguments for repatriating agriculture but there are the interest groups – the NFU, the EEC countries, the City with its investments in land, the chemical companies'.[19] Similarly, one Parliamentary Private Secretary previously critical of the CAP, recalled that 'I am sympathetic to repatriation. If the Germans want to buy votes in Bavaria they should do it themselves. The political power of agriculture is overrated. Even if all the farmers voted against us, we would not lose a single constituency. In a "farming constituency", only 3% of the electorate are farmers'.[20] Nigel Lawson looked ahead to ridding the EEC of the massive distortions caused by CAP subsidies of $22 billion per annum. On top of United States subsidies of $21 billion and Japanese subsidies of $11.8 billion, the agricultural protectionism of the CAP was now the greatest source of conflict in world trade, distorting markets way beyond agriculture. Yet the most imaginative plan that the EEC could suggest was to pay farmers to do nothing by taking land out of production.

Although this would reduce surpluses, the colossal and wasteful cost of subsidies and consequent high food prices would still continue. The Conservative European Reform Group rightly condemned the 'set aside' scheme. Sir Edward du Cann commented that: 'Year after year this sovereign Parliament is expected to aquiesce supinely in this state of affairs and is expected to write another blank cheque. It is high time to say – No, we have had enough'. The Reform Group's statement said that 'We regard such a scheme as a costly nonsense and a device to run away from the problem of overproduction instead of solving it. For a start, it is difficult to see how spending of public money could be justified for paying farmers for producing nothing, unless there is some proof that the resources might be needed some day'.[21] Teddy Taylor has thus convincingly argued that: 'the CAP is interventionist and socialist. It spends £185 million each week; £17 million per week on storage and £5 million per week on destroying food. It costs £11.50 to £13 per week per household. Electorally, it would be wildly popular to reform it. But the Labour Party won't talk about the CAP – Kinnock thought the EEC lost Labour votes in 1983 and won't raise the subject. He wants for the miners what the CAP gives the farmers'.[22]

That Mrs Thatcher shared such sentiments is clear from her antagonism to the CAP. But by the time of the 1987 General Election, the problem was as intractable as ever – if the repatriation option was ruled out. One backbench critic pessimistically assessed the situation: 'Mrs Thatcher has given up on reform of CAP. There is no interest in the media, the Labour party or public opinion and vested interests oppose reform. But there is an explosion coming and in the end farmers will ask for repatriation themselves'.[23]

The 1987 Conservative manifesto promised a 'radical overhaul of the CAP ... to reduce costs and tackle surpluses by bringing supply and demand into better balance'.[24] To achieve this laudable aim in the third term will be a test of Thatcherism in EEC affairs. Until then it is likely that cauliflowers will still be destroyed to keep the price high, EEC butter sold to the Russian consumer at 7p per pound, oranges destroyed or sold on the black market by the Mafia in Italy, and farmers subsidised *not* to produce as well as to produce. The CAP–EEC awaits its deliverance; for if Thatcherism cannot reform it, little else can.[25]

For the British public, Thatcherism in foreign policy is synonymous with a strong defence policy. The Falklands War exemplified
this in the first term and dedication to NATO, including the
possession of nuclear weapons, was its main feature in the second.
In fact, Mrs Thatcher's hostility to the Soviet Union and total
repudiation of unilateralism in any form have been hallmarks of
her foreign policy thinking since before 1979. It was *Pravda* who
nicknamed her 'The Iron Lady' – a sobriquet she has relished –
after speeches in Opposition criticised Soviet aggression and
exploitation of Western goodwill after detente. However, her
policy has been to continue the post-war defence consensus based
on membership of NATO, possession of the British Nuclear
deterrent, and the location of an American (i.e., NATO) nuclear
capacity on British soil. What has focused attention on this policy
and sharpened public awareness of it is the adoption of unilateral
nuclear disarmament by the Labour Party since 1982. Thatcherism
in defence policy has depended on Labour's unilateralism to relate
to the domestic political context.

For a party traditionally associated with the armed forces, this
controversial domestic political aspect has kindled an upgrading of
defence as a priority concern for Conservatives. The party under
Mrs Thatcher's leadership has remained totally committed to the
traditional post-war defence policy consensus. Full support for
NATO is axiomatic, including American nuclear bases on British
soil, and the Polaris independent deterrent is to be replaced by the
Trident system. Even though Mrs Thatcher's leadership remains
unpopular with many on the left of the party, there have been no
criticisms of her defence stance from this quarter. Mr Heath, for
example, who never misses an opportunity to attack the government on the economy, social policy, and EEC affairs, has remained
silent (i.e. in support) on defence and nuclear weapons.

Since 1983, in fact, agreement within the party on defence has
increased. The Falklands lobby is now less vociferous as the
government's determination to garrison the islands has been
demonstrated and the Navy lobby consequently appeased by the
post-Falklands review of John Nott's 1981 Defence Review. The
fledgling 'Gaullist' lobby within the party was effectively emasculated by the promotion of its leading proponent, Alan Clark, into
ministerial office. Thus Mr Clark had to cancel the publication of
an article entitled *Fortress Britain; Graduated moves to strategic*

independence because of the conventions governing ministerial conduct. [26] In recent years the internal party debate on defence has concentrated on financing the various aspects of defence commitments, such as the BAOR or Fortress Falklands, rather than on strategy relating to nuclear weapons.

The Conservatives are clearly confident and happy with their defence stance and, given the contrast with the opposition parties, ever eager to push defence closer than was historically the case to the centre of the political stage. Contrary to other areas of policy, the 1983 Conservative manifesto boasted of increased defence spending and promised to 'maintain our own independent nuclear contribution to British and European deterrence'. [27] In the second Thatcher Government, this policy was resolutely pursued with the party making no apologies for the Trident acquisition. George Younger, the Defence Secretary, has argued that 'only Trident will ensure that our deterrent remains effective'. [28]

At the 1986 Conservative conference, Mrs Thatcher stressed the government policy stance in contrast to the other parties. In her view:

> A Labour Britain would be a neutralist Britain. It would be the greatest gain for the Soviet Union in forty years. And they would have got it without firing a shot. Of course there are fears about the terrible destructive power of nuclear weapons. But it is the balance of nuclear forces which has preserved peace for forty years in a Europe which twice in the previous thirty years tore itself to pieces – preserved peace not only from nuclear war but from conventional war. [29]

During the 1987 Election, the Conservative Party was therefore clearly associated with the fundamental tenets of post-war defence policy and united in rejection of opposition alternatives. The 1987 Conservative manifesto bluntly stated that:

> Labour's policy is to give up Britain's independent nuclear deterrent without asking anything in return. The Labour party would require the United States to withdraw its nuclear weapons from our soil and to close down NATO nuclear bases in Britain. It would remove Britain altogether from the protection of the United States' nuclear umbrella.

The Conservatives' defence policy was thus well known by the electorate and, fortified by Mrs Thatcher's image as a strong leader, the 1983 and 1987 Elections prominently featured defence as an aspect of Thatcherism. In both elections, the reaction of the electorate was remarkably similar. Labour's policy was unpopular and cost the party votes. The Conservatives stressed defence as an issue and devoted a number of televised party broadcasts to the issue. Among Labour's traditional blue-collar voters support for unilateralism remained low; as an issue, it appealed to the party's middle-class activists who dominate the constituency Labour parties. According to Eric Hammond, the leader of the electricians' union and stalwart of Labour's right wing, 'people are refusing to vote Labour because of the defence issue and I didn't find anyone who said they would vote Labour because it is unilateralist'.[30] Hammond's judgement after the 1987 defeat recalled similar comments after the 1983 Election. However, Neil Kinnock has so far ruled out any change in policy, even though 1987 proved a re-run of 1983.

In 1983, the Conservatives, confidently linking strong action in the Falklands War with a strong support for NATO, advocated the traditional post-war defence policy consensus and advocated the modernisation of Britain's nuclear capacity by the acquisition of the Trident missile system. Labour, despite the manifesto's declaration that 'unilateralism and multilateralism must go hand in hand if either is to succeed',[31] was associated with a fully unilateralist, non-nuclear policy which, again according to the manifesto, would be achieved 'over the life time of a Parliament'. As in 1987, Labour strove to combine unilateralism and opposition to NATO strategy with a professed desire to maintain NATO membership. The Alliance in 1983 was committed to multilateral disarmament, but was opposed to Trident, while its adherence to NATO was tempered by 'moving towards a *no first use policy* by strengthening NATO conventional forces' (emphasis in original).[32]

Before the election, it was unknown how the electorate would respond to defence being a high-profile issue in the campaign despite the popularity of the Falklands victory. 1983 was the first election since 1935 when defence was a central, rather than a peripheral, issue. In the event, the supposition of a number of political pundits that defence would be vote-confirmatory, as opposed to an issue of cross-voting, proved incorrect. The Labour

Party was savaged by both Conservatives and the Alliance for leaving Britain neutralist and defenceless and Labour's support among its working-class vote duly fell. The main beneficiary was the Conservative Party, though the Alliance, despite the differences between the Liberal and SDP rank and file, also picked up Labour votes.

Particularly significant in the outcome was that the swing to the Conservatives was higher in constituencies with defence factories or installations. Newbury, for example, where the much-publicised Greenham Common Women's encampment was located, registered the largest single swing to the Conservatives in all 650 seats. Barrow and Furness, usually a safe Labour seat, was won by the Conservatives, who exploited Labour's commitment to cancel the Trident project whose submarines were manufactured in the constituency.

After the 1983 Election there was little evidence to suggest that the British public's opinion on defence matters has changed. Like the parties, the voters, according to opinion polls, entrenched their 1983 position with only marginal changes of perception. Thus the percentage of electors who regard defence–nuclear weapons as the most important issue facing the country has remained steady at between 20 per cent and 30 per cent. In December 1986 it was 26 per cent.[33] If this percentage seems low at first glance, it should be remembered that this is a historically high figure for the post-war period as a whole, and also that only one other issue, unemployment with 78 per cent, ranked higher. Moreover, as serious studies of the correlation of unemployment and voting behaviour have shown, there exists an 'altruistic effect',[34] whereby voters, wishing to appear charitable, answer 'unemployment' to the question ascertaining their views on the most important issue, but answer something quite different when questioned on the issues on which they actually voted. The high unemployment percentage is thus not translated in the polling booths for a vote for the party (Labour) which has traditionally given it greatest priority.

For these reasons, it was no surprise that defence was a major issue in the 1987 election campaign. MORI found that between 25 per cent and 30 per cent of the voters regarded defence as the most important single issue and among all voters it rated in importance only behind unemployment, education and health, and well ahead of law and order, taxation and housing. Moreover, the Conservatives' concentration on defence, while not opening up serious divisions within the Labour Party during the campaign, did produce Mr Kinnock's only major election blunder. When asked innocuously by David Frost to explain his party's policy, Kinnock indicated that a Soviet invasion could be countered by civil resistance. Although he did not actually use the phrase 'guerilla war', that was indeed the sense of his remarks which the Conservatives, and David Owen for the Alliance, seized upon gleefully. It was pointed out that a 'Dad's Army' of resistance was hardly a credible defence policy for an, as yet, undefeated country. Moreover, civilian resistance to Soviet occupation in Hungary and Czechoslovakia had signally failed in 1956 and 1968 respectively. Even when the campaign switched in its later stages to Labour's taxation and industrial relations policies, the Conservatives still found it profitable to return periodically to Labour's unilateralist policy and Mr Kinnock's gaffe to keep the issue on the boil. Thus in 1987 as in 1983 Labour's defence policy was overwhelmingly rejected by the electorate. The Alliance fared little better, particularly after the 1986 Liberal Assembly had rejected the multilateralist stance agreed between Mr Steel and Dr Owen. Thereafter, Alliance defence policy was both split and unconvincing, factors exploited by the Conservatives. George Younger recalled that 'I expected the SDP to be sound on defence, but not the Liberals, who were wedded to CND. Steel was rumbled. He had given support and comfort to the unilateralists which reflected trends in the Liberal party'.[35] Similarly, a Conservative Whip expressed the view that 'My worst nightmare was an Alliance revival in the south of England. The 1986 Liberal Assembly was the turning point. I was surprised how powerful defence was as an issue. You should hear people's views on the council estates'.[36] With both Labour and Alliance vulnerable on defence, the Conservatives duly profited. The scope of Thatcherism in defence policy was therefore unambiguously successful.

Although Mrs Thatcher has aligned the Conservative Party closely to NATO and the United States, and although personal relations with President Reagan have been good, it is a mistaken view to assume a blind pro-Americanism in foreign affairs. Rather, Mrs Thatcher has taken international issues on their merits as they have arisen, placing them in the context of how far they support British interests. Despite the wishes of President

Reagan, Mrs Thatcher withdrew British troops from Belize, irrespective of the turmoil in central America which had prompted Mr Reagan's request that the 1,800 strong garrison should remain. Similarly, Mrs Thatcher expressed reservations about United States armed intervention in Grenada in October 1983. Sir Geoffrey Howe admitted to the Commons that Mrs Thatcher had telephoned the President in a vain attempt to dissuade him from invading a Commonwealth country. Mrs Thatcher also repudiated President Reagan's opposition to the Soviet gas pipeline commercial arrangements, and frequently criticised US economic policy – the high dollar in 1985 and the worsening budget deficit in 1986–7. Even her facilitation of the American bombing raid on Libya in April 1986, by providing British airforce bases, was tempered by a refusal automatically to do so in future. She publicly stated that she hoped that she would not have to receive the same request again. In the wider sense, also, as Pfaltzgraff and Davis correctly argue, the consequences of EEC membership may affect transatlantic defence issues. 'Even under the Thatcher government or another Conservative successor, the United States will confront differences of perspective exacerbated by the transatlantic security issues of the 1990s. They are likely to encompass East–West relations, as well as conflicts in regions outside the North Atlantic area. To the extent that Britain, as a regional power, identifies herself more closely with an evolving European Community, the United States will face the prospect of dealing with an entity that has often sought to establish its identity – and measure its unity – by the distance between its policies and those of the United States'.[37]

On the question of disarmament talks, which featured more prominently after Mr Gorbachev became Soviet party leader, Mrs Thatcher welcomed the negotiations but expressed reservations and caution as to Soviet conventional force levels and the vexed matter of INF verification. Despite her successful visit to Moscow in 1987 and reassurance that the principle of an INF agreement was acceptable, Mrs Thatcher continued to express sufficient doubts as to Soviet intentions to place her alongside Mr Reagan's right-wing critics in Washington, who had viewed the INF negotiations with considerable scepticism. When the prospects for the zero–zero option improved in 1987, Mrs Thatcher reiterated that British nuclear weapons would never be traded away and warned against too great a trust in Soviet long-term global intention. One

Conservative backbench defence specialist considered that 'privately, she's critical of the INF deal and would have preferred a more cautious approach but she felt she couldn't be publicly critical of Reagan and NATO'.[38] She favoured multilateralism, but not at any price. According to Peter Jenkins, she was unhappy with the zero option for intermediate missiles but even less impressed with American notions of ridding the world of nuclear weapons. Allegedly, she gave a hard time to the American Ambassador, Charles Price, demanding to know what difference, if any, there was between Neil Kinnock's and Ronald Reagan's position.[39] The prospect of a non-nuclear Europe – let alone a non-nuclear world – filled her with dread.

Although initially cautious of its effect on the Trident modernisation programme, Mrs Thatcher was subsequently a strong supporter of the SDI, or Star Wars, defence initiative. In December 1985, Britain became the first of America's NATO allies to sign an agreement enabling British companies to participate in the research programme. Mrs Thatcher emphasised the importance of Star Wars at the height of INF negotiations and regarded it as non-negotiable for the West. To be sure, she shared the concern of Star Wars leading to the obsolescence of nuclear weapons and she opposed any denuclearisation which led in that direction. But, as Gerald Frost has argued, despite her reservations, 'there is nothing in the recent behaviour or comments of Mrs Thatcher to suggest that she is anything other than a supporter of SDI.[40]

Finally, Thatcherism in foreign affairs led to friction within the Commonwealth, an international body of largely Third World orientation for which Mrs Thatcher showed little affection. At the 1983 Commonwealth conference, she showed little sympathy for the delegates' preoccupation with South Africa's occupation of Namibia, and the iniquities of the West in not providing sufficient overseas aid. In November 1985, Mrs Thatcher strongly attacked the anti-nuclear policy of the New Zealand Labour Prime Minister, David Lange, who refused to allow nuclear powered or armed ships to visit its ports. But the greatest conflict arose over the desire of the Commonwealth to impose sanctions against the Pretoria regime to hasten the downfall of apartheid. At a meeting at Nassau in October 1985, four Commonwealth leaders – Bob Hawke, Brian Mulroney, Rajiv Ghandi and Kenneth Kaunda – failed to dent her opposition to sanctions. A similar summit in

August 1986 produced the same outcome, although Mrs Thatcher offered to go along with a European Community ban on the import of iron, steel and coal from South Africa. She also accepted a voluntary ban on new investment in South Africa to take effect immediately and she accepted a ban on the promotion of tourism to South Africa.

Full commercial sanctions against South Africa she opposed, leading David Lange to accuse her of protecting Britain's financial interests. As Mrs Thatcher was more concerned with British interests than anything else, it is unlikely that such criticism would have been regarded as anything but a backhanded compliment. This is not to imply that Mrs Thatcher supports apartheid. Geoffrey Howe told the Conservative conference that the continuation of apartheid hastened the possibility of an eventual communist South Africa, a view Mrs Thatcher shared. It was just the case that she could not accept sanctions as the best way of cajoling Pretoria to abandon apartheid by accelerating its reform programme. Mrs Thatcher wanted South Africa to change by persuasion, not by further international isolation and hostility. She felt that a crusade of vilification against the Botha regime would not succeed and might even intensify white reaction, cutting dead any possibilities of reform. Given the misunderstanding of her position and the rupture in the Commonwealth that it provoked, it would be accurate to say that Thatcherism in foreign affairs was far happier dealing with the EEC's budgetary problems or the provision of strong defence.

It was certainly the case that as her second term progressed, Mrs Thatcher seemed to enjoy foreign affairs more, including her visits to Eastern Europe. She developed the capacity to conduct herself well when visiting the Kremlin – 'doing business with Mr Gorbachev', as she put it – and yet to play the anti-Soviet card in domestic politics at home. Cyril Townsend regarded her strategy as more long-term than is usually thought: 'She had been building up to her visit to the Soviet Union for years, sending junior ministers, then the Foreign Secretary and visiting Eastern Europe herself. She prepared the ground extremely well. The success of the relationship with Mr Gorbachev surprised both of them'.[41]

Her aggressive stance to reduce Britain's EEC budget contributions and significantly to reform the CAP could be portrayed as battling for British interests. But equally, Thatcherite nationalism was tempered by realism. The inevitability of the return of Hong Kong to China in 1997 was recognised, and conventional diplomacy appeared to have solved the potential worry of the colony's economic status, as China promised to guarantee capitalism there for at least fifty years. Equally, Mrs Thatcher preferred to co-operate with the Dublin Government through the Anglo–Irish agreement rather than to ally with hardline Unionist opinion. That this policy was maintained after the IRA's failed attempt at assassination in October 1984 at Brighton showed that Mrs Thatcher was not easily deflected in foreign affairs. However, given her very unique style of international leadership, it is unlikely that Thatcherism in foreign policy will survive a future non-Thatcher era.

PART II

The Limits of Thatcherism

CHAPTER 6

The Limits of Thatcherism and the Conservative Party

Mrs Thatcher's leadership – and Thatcherism as a specific ideology – was born from bitter and deep divisions within the Conservative Party in the early 1970s.[1] These divisions simmered up to 1979 and then exploded in the first Thatcher administration in the battle between left and right on economic issues, wets versus dries. By a series of Cabinet reshuffles, Mrs Thatcher outmanoeuvred the wets and by the use of Prime Ministerial power to the full limits of its constitutional propriety, was able to implement her economic strategy despite wet opposition. In the parliamentary party, a large minority wet presence could be counted upon to embarrass the 'monetarist' policies, but was not sufficiently large effectively to challenge them. Only in the party in the country, where the activists in the constituencies supported Mrs Thatcher, were the left wingers in a small enough minority to be discounted. In all, Thatcherism has always faced internal high-level and persistent dissent from within the Conservative Party.

This situation was evident during 1983–7, although the debate shifted to broader philosophical issues away from the technicalities of economic policy or monetary control. Indeed, the nature of the 'wet–dry' debate changed considerably, and was less acrimonious on the backbenches than in the first term. By 1987, the dries had accepted the electoral necessity, at least in the short term, of increasing public spending in politically visible areas such as Health and Education, while the wets had abandoned crude Keynesian reflation and a totally demand management approach to unemployment. A broad synthesis on macro-economic strategy was discernable even though the wet–dry conflict continued over public spending priorities, tax cuts and highly controversial areas

91

of the social security budget. Peter Lilley, Nigel Lawson's PPS recalled that eventually 'the debate fizzled out'[2] and Richard Needham, on the wet spectrum of party opinion, thought 'the argument went away when Lawson had money for both tax cuts and increased public spending. But many things we said in the Blue Chip Group the government did – YTS training and re-training, and a realistic exchange rate. The economic policy arguments have gone but the wet/dry debate over social policy and poverty remains'.[3]

Similarly, Alistair Burt considered that 'as the economy im-proved, the wet/dry debate declined. The wets were rightly trying to convince the government to reduce unemployment. People do not like to think their prosperity is bought at the expense of someone else so tax cuts while unemployment was rising was different from tax cuts after 1986, when unemployment was falling. The wets never acted as a concerted pressure group. 1975, 1979 and 1983 were facts of life and you could not put the clock back. Although I was not 100% convinced of government eco-nomic policy, there could be no return to yesteryear'.[4] One Treasury minister thought 1983 the turning point in the debate once Mrs Thatcher had been triumphantly re-elected: 'the wets began to say spend on infrastructure – that was the word – not just reflate in a neo-Keynesian way. I noticed it strongly in 1987. There was no difference on economic policy as there had been in 1983. The wet/dry division had declined.'[5]

Although a number of left wingers have regarded themselves as chief spokesmen for the wets, the most consistent, and bitter, opponent over the years has been Edward Heath, whom Mrs Thatcher defeated on the first ballot for the leadership in 1975 by only 130 votes to 119. One prominent backbencher commented that 'Heath's never forgiven her for successfully overthrowing him. He forgets that the party was determined to get rid of him and that if it had not been her, it would have been someone else'.[6] Mr Heath's opposition to Thatcherism was as relentless in the second administration as it had been in the first. In January 1984 he led a Commons rebellion over the issue of rate capping, voting with the Opposition on a three line whip for the first time since 1979. He objected to the centralisation of power which he claimed was incompatible with local democracy, conferring draconian powers on central government. Simultaneously, he attacked the government's overall economic record as 'naive and simplistic' with a 'harsh fiscal regime'. He also said that there had been attempts 'to engineer a panic' about public spending and gave a warning against any threat to the Welfare State. 'We can afford to care. We have never been able to afford not to'. As for calls for the privatisation of welfare services, he said that they were in many cases motivated by an unremitting hostility to the state, rather than arguments about efficiency and savings.[7] However, one Conservative whip thought Mr Heath's tactics counter productive, recalling that 'more backbenchers were inclined to support the government if Heath was rebelling. For some time backbench rebellions had been producing diminishing returns. The Conservative Whips office is the most efficient machine I have ever seen. The Whips would know the balance of opinion but what shakes the government is if there is a rebellion from an unexpected source'.[8] By contrast, Mr Heath's rebellions were predictable.

In March 1984, Mr Heath again launched a strong attack on the Prime Minister, accusing her of failing to provide leadership in Europe, using intemperate language and allowing herself to get bogged down in eternal bickering with our European partners. Though the CAP could be criticised, Mr Heath was scathing about the way Mrs Thatcher had gone about it. 'We should remember that our calls for 'reform' when couched in intemperate language are easily caricatured as presaging the destruction of the policy. This is something many of our partners will never accept'.[9] This attack was followed one month later by Mr Heath's accusation that the government was gerrymandering, funking elections and threatening the good name of the Conservative Party with ill-considered, misconceived and unnecessary legislation to pave the way for abolition of the Greater London and Metropolitan Councils. In the Commons debate, he said that 'I am going to vote against tonight's Bill, and so will others on this side of the House and I will say to the Secretary of State quite frankly why. It is a bad Bill and it is paving the way for a worse Bill. There cannot be any justification for this. And immediately it puts the Conservative party open to the charge of the greatest gerrymandering in the last 150 years of British history'.[10] Recalling Mr Heath's attack Patrick Jenkin argued, with much justification, that 'I do not deny that Mr Heath felt strongly about rate capping and GLC abolition. What stuck in my gullet was his accusing us of taking powers that had only ever been taken in wartime. William Waldegrave pointed out that it was Mr Heath who had sought to control by law every wage and price in the country'.[11]

But the government's economic strategy was the subject of Mr Heath's most regular criticism. The long-term Thatcherite policy of cutting taxes, ironically similar to that on which Mr Heath campaigned and had been elected in 1970, was criticised as a neglect of the unemployed. On numerous occasions Mr Heath called for Keynesian reflationary measures and repudiated any supply side incentives such as tax reductions. In November 1985, for example, he stated that tax cuts in present circumstances would be an insult to the employed as well as to the intelligence of the British people and an affront to their integrity. He accused the government of 'financial profligacy' in the disposal of the proceeds of privatisation and ridiculed ministerial claims of a great economic revival. Although Mr Heath's criticisms were so routine as to lose some political impact, they cannot be dismissed as politically irrelevant. They amounted to little in terms of an intellectual criticism of Thatcherism but in the context of the government's opinion poll position trailing Labour, and the mid-term by-election setbacks, Mr Heath's criticisms made life marginally more uncomfortable for the government, ever aware of a public image as 'uncaring' or insensitive to the disadvantaged.

Mr Heath, however, operated as a one-man maverick opposition, a role which another critic of Thatcherism, Francis Pym, wished to avoid. Mr Pym established a conservative ginger group, Centre Forward, to campaign against government economic policies and in favour of a return to consensus Keynesian economics. As Mr Pym advocated in his memoirs, he wished to pursue 'the politics of consent', involving 'more government investment in the public sector ... and the development of an effective regional policy'.[12] Unlike Mr Heath, who had never held a front bench post under Mrs Thatcher, Mr Pym had been Foreign Secretary during the Falklands war and a member of the Cabinet throughout the first term. In June 1983, two days after the election victory, Mr Pym was sacked and returned to the backbenches.

His first rebuttal of government economic policy occurred only two weeks after his dismissal. In the Commons, he attacked the government's attitude to the unemployed, but stopped short, as yet, of calling for a change of policy. He said the first priority should be an imaginative long-term approach to the problem of unemployment. The government must see to it 'that the country never has to make the choice between being divided but rich or united but poor'.[13] Accurately assessing the 'Pym factor', a leader in *The Times* concluded that:

> How much notice will Mrs. Thatcher need to take of Mr. Francis Pym? He demonstrated what an accomplished parliamentarian he is when he addressed the House of Commons on Wednesday for the first time since his dismissal as Foreign Secretary. He may not have been effective as a departmental minister, but as a House of Commons man, he has few superiors. His speech was dignified, arousing sympathy but not overtly courting it. He expressed his loyalty but not to the point where it could be taken for granted. He issued a warning, but not in such openly mutinous terms as to be classed as a rebellion.
> He poses potentially a more formidable threat to Mrs. Thatcher than such dissidents as Mr. Heath or Sir Ian Gilmour have ever done. Mr. Heath has always been too obvious in his resentment; nobody was ever likely to believe that he was acting more in sorrow than in anger. Sir Ian has always seemed more suited to an elegant and principled protest than to mounting an effective rebellion. Mr. Pym is more prudent than Mr. Heath and tougher than Sir Ian.[14]

Mr Pym was also better organised than other principal wets. In a party where pressure groups had abounded – Bow Group, PEST, Selsdon Group, TRG, Monday Club, CARE, and European Reform Group – Mr Pym launched his Conservative Centre Forward in May 1985. The aim was to change policies, not dislodge Mrs Thatcher; the Group were 'loyal' Tories; privatisation and trade-union law reform were *not* under criticism, only economic strategy towards the unemployed. Despite a badly-timed launch and a failure to publish a membership list of MPs, Centre Forward directed public attention to Conservative ideological divisions and prompted a counter-attack from Mrs Thatcher – evidence of the political discomfort the Pym group had initially caused. The Prime Minister mocked the government's 'fair weather friends' and asserted that long-term economic plans would not be diverted for short-term gain. Indeed, as one Thatcherite backbencher remarked, 'Pym's Centre Forward concentrated minds but did not have any impact on government policy. It had a beneficial effect on [the] centre-right which enabled us to organise to counter the enemy in the party'.[15]

The effectiveness of Centre Forward and Mr Pym's style of opposition was never as great after mid-1985. Centre Forward reached its peak with its launch and, after unemployment started to fall steadily from mid-1986, its central purpose lost its main focus. A Conservative Whip commented that 'Centre Forward was not very important. The people supporting Pym were not those who would make us worry'[16] and a Cabinet minister confirmed that 'Centre Forward sank without trace in 3 days. It had no alternative, just the same people advocating that we spend more'.[17] Not all the wets supported Pym's move, particularly the suggestion that voting together would give the group greater coherence. One wet backbencher recalled that 'Pym and Centre Forward was misconceived which was strange as Pym knew how the Party operated. It failed to have any attraction for me once it was suggested it would act together as if whipped in concert'.[18]

Mr Pym himself diverted his criticism to local government policy regarding the rate support grant to shire counties and rarely spoke of Centre Forward only a year after its launch. In 1987 he stood down in his Cambridgeshire constituency, his challenge to Mrs Thatcher and her economic policy exhausted. The Centre Forward episode demonstrated both the scope and limits of Thatcherism: scope in terms of Mrs Thatcher's refusal to adjust her policies and her ability to retain the levers of power, but limits in terms of the opposition she invoked fully ten years after her election as leader. The Conservative left, through Centre Forward, could wound but not destroy her.

Apart from the main challenges of Mr Heath and Mr Pym, the government faced a number of backbench rebellions and isolated examples of ideological strife during 1983–7. The government defeat on MPs' pay, the intensification of the GCHQ row, and the public spending dispute within the Cabinet, contributed to a 'banana skins' period of political embarrassment, during which Conservative opinion poll ratings slumped. One critic within the Cabinet, Peter Walker, urged the Conservative party to indulge less in the ugly rhetoric of economic theory and to move towards the adoption of policies aimed at the creation of full employment.

Emphasising the party's caring role, Mr Walker said 'We must not be content with just freedom under the law. The guiding light in our approach must be a far wider freedom: freedom from Victorian factory conditions; freedom from unemployment'.[19]

Now outside the Cabinet after resigning as Northern Ireland Secretary in September 1984, Jim Prior also expressed similar views. But with his eyes on a business career, Mr Prior's criticisms were reserved largely for his memoirs rather than for the day to day political dispute. Nonetheless, as a senior wet his views were influential, even if unpersuasive to the government. Mr Prior wrote that:

> It is very little compensation that the level of provision for those without jobs is now better than it was in the 1930s. I am deeply concerned that mass unemployment over such a long period is creating a listlessness and a fecklessness in society.
>
> We must do more about unemployment. It is not enough to produce schemes which cope with some of the worst cases and to keep on saying that all a government can do to help is to stick to the same economic policy. There is no reason why our unemployment should be three or four percentage points worse than France or Germany, and with our natural resources of energy we ought to do better.
>
> Many of the schemes for helping the unemployed which have been introduced since the late 1970s were short term, based on the optimistic view that the economy would come right and unemployment would fall. It now looks as if the problem could still be with us for a number of years and we need positive long-term plans to deal with it. Those plans must include full-time education or training for all up to 18, and a much enlarged higher education sector. At the other end of working life, there should be a massive increase in the job release scheme whereby those over 60 can retire if their place is taken by an unemployed person.[20]

Such views were forthcoming from backbench wets also, but it was the specific issue of Sir Keith Joseph's plan to increase parental contributions to student grants by a total of £39 million that proved more damaging for the government. Although there were sound economic reasons for expecting middle-class, better-off parents to pay more, the backbench rebellion encompassed more than just the traditional wets. One hundred and thirty MPs signed motions criticising the proposals and after a stormy meeting of the 1922 Committee, Sir Keith conceded completely, withdrawing the proposed increased contributions. The government also faced a backbench rebellion on implementation of the 1985 Top Salaries Review Body, and criticisms from the left after the Brecon and Radnor by-election debacle in July 1985.

These routine difficulties paled into insignificance in January 1986 when the Westland Affair broke. John Cole has described it as 'the worst personal crisis in Margaret Thatcher's years in Downing Street . . . in the process, she lost two ministers, narrowly stopped her Law Officers from resigning and left her reputation for straight dealing open to attack by her opponents'.[21] One backbench MP recalled that 'Westland was very shaky for the government. I felt the PM could have fallen. On the big occasion, Kinnock blew the debate with a poor speech and from that moment, support began to rally for the PM. Westland was a hothouse issue and the sincerity of the PM was at stake. There has always been a feeling that she was honest and straight and this was put at issue'.[22] 'The crisis was very bad – the worst period of government', said one Cabinet minister[23] and a PPS confessed that 'It took me by surprise. I asked one Cabinet minister about it who said that Heseltine would push it to the limit and the Prime Minister should sack him'.[24]

The public row between two Cabinet ministers, Michael Heseltine's dramatic walk-out from Cabinet and subsequent press conference to announce resignation, and the interminable 'who knew what and leaked to whom' questioning in the Commons all strained the government's reserves of support within the party. Peter Hennessey has observed that:

> By resigning and going public, Heseltine stimulated a crescendo of complaint about the Thatcher style of Cabinet government. Sir Ian Gilmour, sacked from the Cabinet in September 1981, was on both main television news bulletins on 10th January, telling viewers that being a good listener was not one of Mrs. Thatcher's virtues, and that there had been a downgrading of Cabinet government; Cabinet meetings were something to be got through, not the place where views were to be aired and decisions reached.[25]

Yet although the Westland crisis was, in national political terms, disastrous for Mrs Thatcher, as Labour leapt into a twelve point opinion poll lead, the Conservative Party rallied round her leadership surprisingly quickly. The wets were, with some exceptions, reluctant to join the Labour and Alliance orchestration of Commons opposition. This is not to argue that Mrs Thatcher's position was invulnerable. At the height of the crisis, there was speculation that she could fall, which caused some backbench conflict of interpretations as to the seriousness of the crisis. One Tory Whip thought that 'losing two Cabinet ministers is no light matter. I think it damaged the Prime Minister's prestige but it did not linger as long as it might. She is the only blonde who has ever said no to Michael'.[26] Backbench Thatcherites were certainly concerned for Mrs Thatcher's position. One of them recalled that:

> In the wake of Westland, you only needed to look in the Sunday Press to realise that there was somewhere in our ranks, heavy briefing that Margaret cannot survive etc. A good many of us were trying to keep Leon [Brittan] in office because Margaret would be more vulnerable if he went. In the wake of his resignation, the 92 group met to work out how to counter the determined push that as much dirt as possible rubbed off on Margaret. It leaked out that the Whips office had been criticised for not being as supportive of Margaret as it should. I reported to John Wakeham and from then on the threat to Margaret was removed.[27]

Many Conservative MPs, and many a-political members of the public, found the crisis over a medium-sized helicopter company to be blown out of all proportion. The 'who leaked what' debate excited Westminster, but did not long remain in the public mind. As one backbench MP recalled, 'An irrelevant minor matter can be meat and drink to political parties and the Westminster lobby. There was no constituency concern over the Westland helicopter company. Brittan's resignation seemed inevitable even though it was an unfair situation for him'.[28] Mrs Thatcher told a TV interviewer that 'Westland is a small thing and had it not been for the fact that we had one member of the team who was not playing as a member of the team, this would never have arisen', and Home Secretary, Douglas Hurd, said he saw the Westland affair as a 'little stream which suddenly flash-flooded its banks and swept away two ministers and did a lot of damage'. But it would get back in the right channel and it was overwhelmingly in the national interest that it should do so.[29] Similarly, a senior backbench MP thought 'Today's crisis is tomorrow's odd affair. It was stupid and idiotic and we drifted into it. Heseltine's a loner and I think he resigned on impulse',[30] while a Cabinet minister ventured that 'there was a little bit of play acting in Heseltine's resignation'.[31] Given the hasty and bitter Press conference which followed Mr Heseltine's resignation, it is not unfair to point out that he sought to dramatise the crisis. As another Cabinet minister remembered it 'There was no vote in Cabinet over Westland. Heseltine said he could not accept that statements had to be submitted for approval on government policy. She [Mrs Thatcher] said "I am very sorry, let's order some coffee, complete the item and have a break". Heseltine walked out and when I left the meeting, was giving his press conference'.[32]

Nevertheless, the fact remained that the Westland Affair had damaged Mrs Thatcher's political stature and that now Michael Heseltine was added to the list of internal party opponents able to speak out freely from the backbenches against government economic policy. Touring the constituencies, Mr Heseltine advocated industrial strategies, attacked laissez-faire economics, and placed a firm priority on government intervention to stimulate employment especially in the inner cities. In a book outlining his philosophy, Mr Heseltine, moving beyond the thinking of traditional wets, advocated experimentation with American style schemes of 'workfare', suggesting that:

> Those who live amid dereliction do not need to have it pointed out that there is plentiful scope for useful work to be organised in their communities from which all would gain. If the Government commits itself, as I have urged, to greatly increased expenditure on urban renewal, there will be a response. If devastated sites are cleared and homes made habitable and gardens planted, I believe the able-bodied unemployed, if wisely led, will join in and make their contribution with pride.[33]

The Heseltine factor could not be ignored in the wake of Westland, given his wider popularity in the party which many wets had never sufficiently cultivated. Indeed, as Heseltine's sympathetic biographer, Julian Critchley, has commented, 'Heseltine had never been closely identified with Mrs Thatcher's opponents'[34] which may account for his popularity. However, it would be an exaggeration to see Mr Heseltine's action as an immediate leadership bid. As one junior minister put it 'Heseltine wasn't making a leadership bid. It was his pan-European views that were important'.[35] In the longer term, of course, Mr Heseltine may well have had leadership ambition, but that also applies to many Cabinet ministers and is an occupational hazard Prime Ministers must contend with.

Westland also made Mrs Thatcher vulnerable to backbench dissent, as was demonstrated by the British Leyland sell-off climbdown described in Chapter 4. Similarly, backbench opposition killed one of the most important Thatcherite reforms – Britain's outdated Sunday Trading laws – in the wake of Westland. Following the report of the Auld committee in 1984, the then Home Secretary, Leon Brittan announced the government's intention of liberalising the Sunday Trading laws, backed by a Commons motion signed by a hundred backbenchers favouring deregulation. Although the Bill was expected to have a rough passage, given the combination of the religious lobby and the wets, there was little expectation, before Westland at least, that it would be defeated. Both Mrs Thatcher and Douglas Hurd, the Home Secretary in charge of the legislation, favoured a total deregulation and were reluctant to allow amendments that would have emasculated the Bill. Mr Hurd even threatened to abandon the Bill in a bid to break Conservative backbench opposition, in the hope that some critics would then relent. A number of local authorities had for some time turned a blind eye to shops which opened on a Sunday and public opinion supported greater shopping freedom.

The government expected that some backbenchers would not wish to vote with Labour – who opposed Sunday trading in deference to the shop workers' union USDAW – in suppressing a popular measure. These expectations turned out to be false. Sufficient backbenchers, for a variety of different reasons, voted with the opposition parties to defeat the Bill and an important Thatcherite deregulation measure was lost. Whether the outcome would have been the same had Westland not weakened the government is open to speculation. The backbench rebellion had demonstrated the limits of Thatcherism and the vulnerability of radical legislation to an organised backbench challenge. Peter Jenkins shrewdly argued that 'the incident revealed the difficulties of modernising Britain. It revealed once more, the power of producer interests over the silent majority of consumers. It showed how easy it was for small numbers of people determined to oppose change to frustrate the will of the reformer, especially when they were equipped with word processors'.[36] Similarly, one backbench MP bemoaned that 'I was always in favour of it and it was in the party manifesto. There was a well orchestrated lobby of letters written by local churches which influenced a lot of my colleagues'.[37] It may be pointed out, though, that as more shops defy the law and open on Sunday, the Thatcherite solution may come about *de facto* if not *de jure* irrespective of the strength of parliamentary opposition.

While the defeat of the shops Bill marked the last substantial successful backbench rebellion of the parliament, the government was still attacked by its Conservative critics up to and including the 1987 General Election. Peter Walker urged a radical rethink of economic policy if a third election victory was to be achieved and envisaged a Britain caught in a 'long term, relentless, remorseless decline'. On the economy, he argued that

> There can be no complacency by a Tory government towards unemployment. Three and a half million people having to be paid billions of pounds of benefits to produce nothing offends the pride of our country. In the last election they gave us the benefit of the doubt. We will not obtain any such benefit next time. Not everything can be left to market forces. If other governments stand shoulder to shoulder with their industries then we have no alternative but to do the same.[38]

Another emerging dissident, though regarded as an unlikely one, was leader of the House, John Biffen. He speculated about the need for the Tories to go into the 1987 Election on a balanced ticket. The Prime Minister had both qualities and liabilities, he said. And nobody supposed she would remain Prime Minister for the whole of a third term. So what was needed was a team approach of Thatcher and other top Tories, 'one of whom probably would become prime minister in due course'.[39] Downing

Street dismissed the remarks, adding that Mr Biffen was a 'semi-detached member of the Government', a reference to Mr Biffen's habit of independent thinking aloud. Despite impressive Thatcherite credentials as a free-marketeer and opponent of incomes policy and Keynesianism in Mr Heath's administration, Mr Biffen had become disillusioned with Thatcherism, fearing that it had made Toryism 'a raucous political faction'. He favoured consolidation rather than further radicalism. Speculation that his remarks amounted to a bid for the party leadership were off target, but that served only to make his criticism more stinging. During the 1987 election campaign, Mr Biffen made pessimistic predictions as to the election outcome, distancing himself from the official Conservative campaign in a way reminiscent of his one-time mentor, Enoch Powell, who had done the same in 1970. Not surprisingly, following Mrs Thatcher's return to office in June 1987, Mr Biffen suffered a similar fate to Francis Pym, being swiftly despatched to the backbenches.

Viewed overall, the years 1983–7 saw a continuation of the ideological strife which had marked the first Thatcher term, albeit at a lower level of animosity or dispute. While Mrs Thatcher can be deemed to have 'won' the internal battle by virtue of Cabinet reshuffles, the exercise of her Prime Ministerial authority, and her inviolate position as leader unchallenged under party rules, the senior levels of the Conservative Party still cannot be counted as Thatcherite. The unrepentant wets are a minority but a sizeable and disruptive one. In many ways, they are akin to the old Empire right wing of the party in the 1950s, which never accepted decolonisation and 'winds of change' in Africa. Vocal, determined, embittered at the Suez fiasco, they lost the battle within the party but left their mark on two decades. The wets of the Thatcher era are in a similar position. Outnumbered, they are reluctant to go for the jugular and openly dispute the leadership by election. Vocal, determined, and like Mr Heath, embittered, they skirmish and ambush individual Thatcherite policies such as local government rates reform or Sunday Trading. However, 'hardcore' wets are fewer on the ground as the wet–dry division of the first term declined. One dry backbencher recalled:

A good deal of the economic argument on the backbenches was changing. The demarcation line was between those who wanted to cut spending and others who wanted more for infrastructure. Part way through the parliament, we found people arguing for both, which took the pressure from the old wet/dry conflict. The wets had lost the intellectual argument. A number of ministers whom we had considered wet were embracing a radical Tory policy – Ken Baker at education and Ken Clarke embracing with all fervour, the possibilities for privatisation'.[40]

But another backbench dry provided a different analysis. Teddy Taylor argued that 'this government has been pursuing wet policies. We have stopped the increased share of public sector in terms of GNP but not reversed it. Demand led social spending has risen, paid for by asset sales, higher growth and oil'.[41] This maverick view is at variance to the wider picture of wet abandonment of Keynesianism, incomes policies and industrial interventionism with which they had approached the second term. Although there was a synthesis of views, the dries appeared to have won the intellectual battle. In losing the overall, long-term, ideological battle – inherent in Mr Heath's 1975 leadership election defeat, perhaps – the diehard wets reveal the extent of Thatcherism; but in constantly opposing it, occasionally with acute political embarrassment, they reveal Thatcherism's limits as well.

Aside from relatively trivial disagreements – for example, concerning the merits of rival advertising agencies for use in general elections[42] – Mrs Thatcher was able to rely upon a number of senior Thatcherite ministers to provide political ballast for the second term. Norman Tebbit, Nigel Lawson, Sir Geoffrey Howe, Lord Young, Nicholas Ridley and John Moore all embraced the fundamental ideological nature of a combative Thatcherism rolling back the years of socialism. All saw the government's policies in the longer-term wider framework of encouraging a free enterprise, entrepreneurial society, liberated from constraints of trade-union power, nationalised inefficiency and higher taxation chasing higher public spending. Similarly, on the backbenches a loyal group of Thatcherites could be relied upon to counter the arguments of the Conservative left. Yet Thatcherism has also had to rely upon the support or acquiescence of those in the centre of the party or those sufficiently ambitious not to allow their wet tendencies to dampen their career advancement. The administration as a whole, as represented by the ministerial and PPS payroll vote, displayed a balance between different Conservative perspectives.

Whether Kenneth Baker, Kenneth Clarke, Douglas Hurd, Norman Fowler and George Younger are classified as closet wets, semi-Thatcherites, pragmatists or just plainly ambitious for themselves and their party is immaterial. Such people have proved invaluable to the longevity of Thatcherism and to Mrs Thatcher's entrenched position as leader. But equally they could prove eager advocates of quite different policies in a post-Thatcher era. Thatcherism, therefore, is not sufficiently dominant in the party fully to survive the political obituary of its founder. Such an analysis should not be contentious. Conservatism has always been adaptable – without adaptability, Mrs Thatcher could not have become leader. While the Conservative Party has often been associated with particular ideologies – imperial expansion, Keynesian political economy and Thatcherism to name but three – it has never been associated with any single ideology for all time. The Conservative Party has no equivalent of an ideological holy grail, Clause IV style. This has enabled ideology to change with society and to mould itself to the requirements of a mass 20th-century electorate.

Thatcherism, therefore, is likely one day to pass into the party's history and collective memory just as surely as did the belief that the British Empire would last for ever, or that Macmillan-style Keynesianism would permanently keep the party in office. Dennis Kavanagh has even gone as far as to suggest that there may be a reaction to Mrs Thatcher's forcefulness and style, so that 'instead of having a successor who carries on her work, she may find that her retirement is a sign that public opinion and politicians are once again seeking a conciliatory and emollient leader'.[43] While such an outcome cannot be ruled out, its immediate prospect was not visible during 1983–7, with the brief exception of the worst moments of the Westland crisis. Nor may it be visible for some years to come. After all, the Conservative Party embraced the post-war Keynesian consensus for thirty years before abruptly ditching its most devoted adherent Edward Heath. Mrs Thatcher herself will not be Prime Minister for thirty years but a neo-Thatcherism, given the right political climate within the party, could prosper under a leader of similar views.

The success, or otherwise, of Thatcherism within the Conservative ideological kaleidoscope has depended, and will continue to do so, on electoral victories. As John Cole has written:

> Mrs. Thatcher has what football goalkeepers call a clean sheet, and she will want to keep it that way, to go into history as one political leader in this century who has been in charge for a long time, yet has never been defeated. Her strengths as Prime Minister and party leader have been an ability to win votes; an unremitting appetite for hard work; a mind and instinct for political decisions and pitfalls that have usually been as sharp as razors; a shell like a tortoise, into which she can withdraw as the missiles fly around her; an ability not to be bored by her own habit of repetition, of hammering out, again and again, the arguments that suit her – higher production, lower inflation, more home-owners, more shareholders, and so on.[44]

Such a style suits a party that regards general election victories as almost a precondition for its existence and survival. The Conservative Party is nothing if not the party of office – the natural party of government, as it has often proclaimed. Perhaps this is a bottom line political fact of life that will make or break the wets. The more general election victories Mrs Thatcher achieves, the weaker their position becomes in terms of reversing her hold on power. The Conservative Party is known to be brutal with failed leaders. Of recent leaders, only Churchill had the authority to retain the leadership after an election defeat. But, equally, it is a party which rewards leaders who win with a loyalty that Labour (and Alliance) leaders can only envy. While Thatcherism delivers office to the Conservative Party, it is likely to prosper. As Philip Norton observes, 'Mrs. Thatcher enjoys the loyalty and support of the party which she leads. However, that support is contingent, not certain'.[45] The left-wing Conservative opponents of Thatcherism can expect defeat to reveal its limits. But, as will be discussed in Chapter 9, the 1983–7 government ended its term of office with a renewed mandate of a 101-seat majority.

CHAPTER 7

The Limits of Thatcherism and the British Left

In conventional political terms, the policies of the Thatcherite years based on convincing election victories have dealt a devastating blow to the British left. The scope of Thatcherism in rolling back the post-war consensus and in winning votes from a new generation of home-owners and share investors has shattered the left's hope of immediate political power. Moreover, the division of the left between Labour and the Alliance has split the anti-Conservative vote to the left's clear electoral disadvantage. All these facets of the Thatcher years have demonstrated the left's failures after an era in which Labour won four out of five elections. The mood on the left has consequently been one of self-re-examination and gloom, punctuated by the odd by-election victory. All these aspects of Thatcherism, as this account has argued, are self-evident of the assault on collectivism.

But in another sense the British left, while it has not prevented or defeated Thatcherism, has been able to limit it. The left has not been able to prohibit Thatcherite legislation or economic policy, but it has restricted its acceptance to a minority of the population. Whereas the Attlee Government in 1945–51 created the post-war consensus which lasted, across all political parties, until 1979, the Thatcherite consensus has been confined to the Conservative Party – excluding the diehard wets – and the followers of Dr David Owen. A new consensus has not emerged since 1979, despite the dismantling of the socialistic, collectivist, Keynesian, corporatist consensus which preceded it. Thatcherism has triumphed but not convinced. Sufficient numbers of people have stuck to either Labour Party socialism or Alliance consensus Keynesianism to deny Thatcherism a majoritarian consensus.

The Labour Party has scarcely embraced one single aspect of

107

Thatcherite reform. It has opposed every single privatisation, promising in some cases, renationalisation or social ownership. It opposed council house sales and only reluctantly dropped the policy because it lost votes. Labour has denounced all deregulation and economic liberalisation from competitive tendering in local government to liberalising coach and bus routes. Labour has voted against all tax cuts and attempts to control public spending despite the fiscal rectitude of the Callaghan Government when faced with the IMF. Labour's approach to the growing private sector has varied between reluctant toleration and outright hostility. The growth in self-employment has escaped praise. Labour has sought to reiterate its belief in public ownership and collective provision, direction of investment by way of an industrial strategy, and the belief that government spending can reduce unemployment. Only one or two fringe voices – Austin Mitchell, for example – have been prepared to move beyond a grudging toleration of private enterprise to an open approval. In what was regarded as a speech seeking a policy review, Mr Kinnock, at Labour's 1987 conference, stated that Labour was not hostile to private industry – but he could not bring himself wholeheartedly to commend it.

While it may be true to say that Neil Kinnock has moved Labour policy rightwards from that inherited from Michael Foot in October 1983, the Kinnock party is still way to the left of the Wilson and Callaghan Governments. The march of the middle-class, public-sector employed activists in the party – the lumpen polytechnica rather than the lumpen proletariat – has continued to such an extent that a reversion to the trade-union based moderate Labour Party of the Gaitskell–Wilson period is now a sociological impossibility.[1] First discerned in the late 1960s by sympathetic writers such as Hindess,[2] the success of the left's middle-class hard left has been recently chronicled by Crick[3] and Kilroy-Silk.[4] Following the introduction of mandatory re-selection of MPs, the PLP is steadily beginning to resemble the Constituency Labour Parties (CLPs) as more activists are selected. This process for the first time gave the left a majority over the right in the PLP after the 1987 Election. In policy terms, this development may well render support for Clause IV socialism a stronger aspect of party ideology than Neil Kinnock's limited policy re-appraisal. Far from seeking an accommodation with Thatcherism the Labour Party, as a whole, may well drift further away from accepting an entrepreneurial, enterprise economy. All these aspects of Labour policy are in keeping with the party's tradition, constitution and principles. They are assimilated within the British tradition of democratic socialism.

Brian Walden has pointed out that a loathing of the market, choice and economic individualism are very much the hallmarks of the current generation of Labour Party Socialists, particularly in local government. Indeed, such a hatred of 'capitalism' is the very source of ideological commitment of Labour Party members. Whether or not electoral considerations may lead to a tempering of such views in public, in private they remain a potent source of utopian Socialist idealism. Once the Labour Party had irrevocably split in 1981, it lost any influx of social democratic, mixed-economy advocates. The motivating force of the current entrants into the party consists essentially of an anti-capitalist, anti-market critique, ultimately envisaging a fundamentally Socialist economy. While Neil Kinnock retains the leadership with such certainty, the party's hard left can be frozen from the policy process, as was evident in the drawing up of the 1987 election manifesto. But time is on the side of the hard left in the 1990s, just as it was on Kinnock's side in the 1970s. This feature of Labour ideology is likely to preclude any approval – as opposed to reluctant acceptance – of a market-oriented economy.

However, in other countries of differing political and economic systems, parties of the left have made moves towards a greater acceptance of markets, privatisation or other policies which in the British context are Thatcherite. In France, Spain, Italy and Portugal the Socialist parties have embraced the notion of a primarily market economy. In New Zealand, David Lange's ruling Labour Party has privatised and deregulated one of the most cossetted and restrictive economies of the Western World. In Australia, Bob Hawke's Labour Party has deregulated the financial markets, supported privatisation and a vigorous private sector. Business support for Mr Hawke has increased and his three consecutive election victories are testimony to his party's popularity. Japan, whose domestic economy is far less impressive than is supposed, has privatised state industries to improve efficiency and customer choice, and India under Rajiv Gandhi's bold leadership has begun the process, albeit slowly, of lifting numerous restrictions on enterprise.

In Eastern Europe, ruling Communist parties have made moves towards the greater use of market forces. Mr Gorbachev in the Soviet Union has introduced *perestroika*, or economic re-structuring, to involve – for the first time since the 1920s – limited private enterprise; self-employment in some areas has actually been legalised from 1 May 1987. In Hungary, market reforms have provided the highest standard of living in the Eastern bloc, the economy openly described as 'market socialism'. Bulgaria has sold public housing to its tenants to encourage home-ownership and East Germany has expanded its private agricultural sector. China has long since discarded the Socialist path of Maoism in favour of market reforms, though in deference to ideology, this process is called simply 'modernisation'. A stock exchange has opened in Shanghai and new economic zones flourish.

In other countries, too, similar reforms have occurred. Argentina has introduced privatisation to break the stranglehold of corrupt state-run industries and Mexico has privatised 67 industrial concerns. Colonel Gadaffi in Libya has reversed his policy of exterminating private enterprise after it resulted in food shortages and widespread discontent. Uganda, Ghana and even Tanzania have experimented on a limited scale with market reforms. Of course some countries are still adamantly opposed to any private sector development – Romania, the Malagasy Republic, Nicaragua, Cuba and Ethiopia. The British Labour Party lies in between. It has yet to welcome a growing private sector including privatisation and increased home-ownership. But it has realised the futility in electoral terms of outright opposition. The result is that Labour's leadership has adopted a stance of toleration or reluctant acquiescence in the abstract concept of the market economy while opposing specific privatisations and deregulation proposals. While Socialist writers such as Seyd[5] are correct to distinguish between the extensive socialist transformation envisaged by the (hard) left, as opposed to the reformism of the Kinnock leadership, it still remains the case that the Labour leadership would *not* favour any moves towards a more private sector-oriented economy. Indeed, Kinnock's reformism has never suggested any Gaitskellite attempt to ditch the Clause IV commitment to the abolition of capitalism. Kinnock's sympathetic biographer, Michael Leapman, has suggested that Kinnock would be happy to abandon *de facto* but not *de jure* Clause IV policies. Until grudging toleration of the market sector can be transformed into approval it is difficult, if not impossible, to imagine the Labour Party as anything but intellectually opposed to the market. This reaction places the Labour Party well to the left of its European or antipodean counterparts, and has prevented the emergence in Britain of any new consensus based on Thatcherite economic change.

The Alliance, prior to its fatal rupture after the 1987 Election, was divided on how to react to Thatcherism. The Liberals under David Steel's leadership were never hostile to a successfully functioning market economy. But they could not bring themselves to embrace privatisation, preferring to call for a truce on ownership of industry, freezing the public and private sector boundaries. However, Liberal economic policy was firmly rooted in the postwar Keynesian consensus. Every Liberal election manifesto since 1966 called for Keynesian reflation accompanied by a planned long-term incomes policy (as opposed to the *ad hoc* panic incomes policies of the period). This policy stance continued unchanged into the 1980s, although the method of incomes policy control was reshaped to include an inflation tax on employers paying above the specified 'norm'. This incomes policy was sold not, as more sophisticated Keynesians would argue, as a way of reducing unemployment, but as a method of having reflation without inflation. It is difficult to envisage an overall macro-economic strategy more alien to Thatcherism.

The Alliance manifesto in 1987 promised legislative powers to enforce incomes restraint and David Steel, during the campaign, seemed to flirt with a coalition with Labour but to rule out one with Mrs Thatcher. Mr Steel put it that 'the ideology of Thatcherism must be driven out . . . the new right in the Conservative party have taken one nation and split it into two'.[6] Other Liberal politicians took a similar line, with only former leader, Jo Grimond, tempted to praise aspects of Thatcherism. David Owen and the SDP were much more sympathetic to the intentions and underlying intellectual thrust of Thatcherism. At the 1983 SDP conference, Dr Owen was challenging the viability of strict incomes policy and soon began to use the phrase the 'social market economy' as a description of a more market economy better capable of the relief of poverty and redistribution of wealth.

Although Owen's social market economy would have 'some form of incomes policy . . . to reduce unemployment without triggering inflation',[7] this aspect was not stressed with the same conviction inherent in the Liberal's approach. Dr Owen welcomed privatisation in principle, though critical of transferring public monopolies to private monopolies, and fully supported notions of home- and share-ownership.

But by 1987, the Alliance manifesto was bereft of any mention of the social market and criticism of Thatcherism and Socialism were distributed in roughly equal measure. Thatcherism was rejected in favour of the middle way, with a grand coalition of the left in a hung parliament a possible option. Linked to the Liberal rank and file preference for unilateralism, the 1987 Alliance economic policy was too remote from Thatcherite change to persuade Dr Owen to join a merged Liberal–SDP Party following the 1987 General Election. In September 1987 Dr Owen and the SDP supporters who rejected any merger finally advocated a neo-Thatcherite policy stance, accepting privatisation, a market economy, trade union law reform and the possession of a British nuclear deterrent. But as only 43 per cent of SDP members had voted not to merge with the Liberals – and not all of those preferred an *outright* opposition to any merger – Dr Owen's attempt to create an opposition to the Conservatives which tacitly accepted Thatcherism had failed. With the exception of an Owenite rump, Thatcherism has persuaded few people on the British left to accept its merits, let alone to steal its clothes. Both Labour and the merged Liberal–SDP Party maintain a strong anti-Thatcherite intellectual position, looking to reverse Thatcherism in the future rather than build upon it. In failing favourably to come to terms with the central tenets of Thatcherism, the British left has retained the capacity to limit it – if the left can regain power, that is.

The left has gained power in the Thatcher years at local level, and this has occasioned a furious conflict between local authorities claiming a local mandate for Socialism and the government claiming a mandate nationally for controlling public expenditure in accordance with Britain's traditional unitary state. This conflict was evident in the first Thatcher term and intensified in 1983–7. The government's problems have stemmed from the fact that the old definitions of *ultra vires* which decreed what local government had to do and could not do, was effectively swept away by the 1972

Peter Walker reforms. Consequently, a series of legal ambiguities has developed over the scope and function of local authorities. No longer can local authorities be prevented from doing anything that does not conflict with national law. The scope of local government functions, services and policies has mushroomed, causing financial chaos and budgetary profligacy. The GLC was in the vanguard of the new municipal socialism. Peter Jenkins has described Ken Livingstone's policy of spending money as an 'antidote to monetarism':

> By giving money to special interest groups, and funding all manner of leftie and loony causes, a motley coalition of minorities was assembled. Blacks, feminists, Irish, gays, disabled, one-parent families, welfare claimants, homeless, peace campaigners – all were identified as potential recruits to the new ersatz proletariat which would reinforce the thinning ranks of the workers. The GLC hired more and more people to give more and more money to more and more people. In 1983–4, it handed out £42 million, in 1984–5 £47 million. To give away the money, it hired the same sort of people it was giving the money to, although in truth only a small proportion of the money went to the exotic causes which got into the newspapers.[8]

Such policies, however produced bizarre anomalies. It is legal, for example, for local authorities to pursue their own foreign and defence policies as many of them do, by declaring nuclear-free zones and hiring 'peace officers' to patrol them. But, as Mrs Thatcher has told the Commons, such policies have no status in law. Public money is therefore needlessly wasted. It was legal for local authorities to donate public money to assist the NUM during the 1984–5 strike; it is legal for local government to donate money for political purposes to ethnic or minority groups such as homosexuals. Provided the correct procedures are followed in committee and the money allocated in accordance with accepted accounting methods, local government has near total freedom to spend money on any policy hostile to and incompatible with that of the elected government at Westminster. Pat Seyd's study of the Labour left shows how in Sheffield the ruling Labour groups could effectively 'aim to reform local social relations by establishing alternative forms of organisation which challenge the market economy: for example, the establishment and encouragement of worker co-operatives and by employing its own direct labour force'.[9]

Hitherto, successive Environment Secretaries have treated the local government problem as one of aggregate or total spending. But, important though that is, it misses the point of the political and ideological conflict between the left and the government. What is vital for the left is its ability to spend money on causes of its own choosing. The money donated to the miners' strike fund did not infringe the government's guidelines, provided the aggregate spending total was not exceeded. Nicholas Ridley has thus argued that 'Local government had been allowed to stray from its functions. All local government powers are derived from parliament and parliament has to lay down what local government should do'.[10]

The left has therefore had considerable success in limiting Thatcherism at local level.[11] Towards the end of the 1983–7 parliament, ministers often referred to the 'loony left' in local government, donating money to ever more esoteric pressure groups. The public disquiet over such spending affected the general election in the London area where 'loony left' councils had become unpopular. However, the question that should be asked is how and why the government had permitted such types of spending in the first place. After eight years of Thatcherism, no action had been taken to make such spending illegal (as it was before 1972). The abolition of local authority discretionary spending had been fudged by the government, which allowed discretionary spending and then publicly ridiculed it for party political purposes. The 1987 Conservative manifesto tamely noted that 'the abuses of left-wing Labour councils have shocked the nation',[12] but failed to suggest any remedy save those – such as the Community charge – which affect only total spending, not its component parts. Of course, tackling the rates burden and re-structuring local authority finance are laudable enough aims (even if the Community charge is given the benefit of the doubt) but they do not tackle the source of the left's power to obstruct and counter government policy. That power derives from the ability to allocate public money to a variety of causes which directly work against the allocation of public money nationally. The politicisation of local government follows directly from this power with the interest in traditional areas of local spending – roads, street lights, libraries, etc. – downgraded in the quest for local socialism. A return to a strict *ultra vires* system, stipulating what local authorities can, and cannot, do would end politicisation at a stroke. If Thatcherism aims at the extinction of Socialism, that must imply the ending of local Socialism which thrives on discretionary spending and politicisation. It was ironic that the government should legislate against and surcharge Labour's councillors for breaching aggregate spending limits, not for what they had spent money on. The implication that as long as total spending targets are met it does not matter where the money is allocated, has allowed the left successfully to frustrate Thatcherism at a municipal level. Patrick Jenkin had defended the government's policy of not tackling the question of how local government money is spent by arguing that 'we could not have legislated on abuses. We had a reputation for authoritarianism and intolerance which was doing the party damage. If I had stepped in and banned certain spending, I would have got a muddy stick in the eye. I set up Widdicombe so we could be absolutely sure'.[13] But arguably the establishment of Widdicombe only delayed tackling the problem, and public opinion would have been unlikely to oppose a government seen to be correcting abuses of local government spending power. By failing to tackle the real local government opposition, the government blundered through 1983–7, using a variety of attacks on the left.

Abolition of the GLC and the Metropolitan councils was the first policy. The process of abolition turned into a dog's breakfast of complications for the government. An elected body was to be replaced by non-elected ones, leaving the government open to charges of acting undemocratically. Functions of the GLC were often transferred to boroughs, many of whom were as wasteful and as politicised as the GLC itself. Ken Livingstone, the GLC leader, was transformed from a scarcely popular local government party chief into a national political figure, defying the government by using public money to attack its policies in a series of advertisements. GLC elections were cancelled and backbench Conservative rebellions commonplace. The House of Lords gave the abolition Bill an uncharacteristically rough ride. To be sure, abolition did confer some advantages from a government viewpoint. A costly layer of bureaucracy was dismantled – particularly in the metropolitan counties – and obvious abuses such as the artificial jobs created at public expense by the Greater London Enterprise

Board (GLEB) removed. But overall, the government's victory was a pyrric one; and local government was just one of many battles. The government's blunderbus approach to the GLC missed the real targets of politicisation and waste. As David Walker put it:

> On one side is a benign public authority which helps keep life in the capital civilised. It runs the computer that makes the traffic lights change colour in sequence along the Cromwell Road, renews the gaskets on the fire brigade's pumps, replaces the lavatorial tiles along the Rotherhithe Tunnel, promotes Purcell at the Queen Elizabeth Hall and screws up blue plaques to dead dignitaries. The other GLC is sometimes less visible, but often much more controversial. It spends large sums on 'planning', shuffles public money from ratepayers to the London Lesbian and Gay Centre, and meets on the third Tuesday of the month in a Parliament-sized debating chamber to bicker and swop rhetoric between the parties in front of half a dozen yawning members of the public...
>
> Stop the Kenwood open air concerts on warm June evenings and middle-class amenity suffers; close down the Woolwich Ferry and a lifeline in a neglected part of south-east London is cut. But abolish the job of the 'chief economic planner' and who will care? End those County Hall shenanigans that pass for local democracy at work and how many Londoners will even register the fact?[14]

Similarly, the government's long-running war with the Militant-controlled Liverpool City council, effectively run not by council leader John Hamilton but by his ubiquitous deputy, Derek Hatton, led to the same difficulties. The concentration was not on the council's spending as such but on its breach of total spending limits and subsequent inability to set a rate. Patrick Jenkin backed down initially in this battle and eventually the government legislated to surcharge councillors who had wilfully overspent. But the removal of Hatton and his supporters did not end the problem, as fresh elections brought to power another Labour council committed to politicisation and defiance of national government policies – for example, by opposing all manifestations of private enterprise. It is a testimony to the government's failure to deal convincingly with

Liverpool that the most effective attack on Mr Hatton was made
by Neil Kinnock at the 1985 Labour conference. Mr Kinnock's sympathetic biographer, Michael Leapman, described Mr Kinnock as
attacking extremism in his own party:

> You start with far-fetched resolutions. They are then pickled
> into a rigid dogma, a code, and you go through the years sticking
> to that, out-dated, misplaced, irrelevant to the real needs, and
> you end in the grotesque chaos...
> – now he was raising his voice until he was nearly shouting,
> and excited murmurs were already rippling through the hall –
> ... the grotesque chaos of a Labour council – a *Labour* council –
> hiring taxis (he almost spat the word) to scuttle around a city
> handing out redundancy notices to its own workers.
> There was uproar. The TV cameras zoomed in on the
> audience to locate Hatton shouting 'lies' above the hubbub.
> Suddenly they switched back to the platform, just in time to see
> Eric Heffer, staring blankly ahead of him, climb from the stage,
> walk to the back of the auditorium and out through the doors.
> Nobody could remember any similar walkout by an NEC
> member during the leader's speech and the noise grew louder as
> left-wingers applauded Heffer and booed Kinnock, while loyal-
> ists raised counter-cheers for the leader.[15]

Mr Kinnock's speech marked the end of Mr Hatton's political
career more effectively than any ministerial policy towards Liverpool. For example, the banning and surcharging of councillors
proved a short-term solution, as one set of municipal socialists
would replace the other, continuing almost identical policies. In
dealing with Derek Hatton, Patrick Jenkin recalled that:

> Hatton threatened me with violence to my London home. Some
> of my officials were stunned. They had never heard the Secre-
> tary of State threatened with violence in a meeting before. I had
> to have police protection. Cunningham and Straw regarded
> Hatton as a crook but Kinnock thought that any stick to beat the
> government will do... It was the law that tamed Hatton, not
> Kinnock. I said that the law would not be impotent and in the
> end will catch up with you.[16]

The law did indeed catch up with Mr Hatton, but not with the abuse of spending power by the municipal left. The Liverpool problem was still unsolved at the start of the third Thatcher term. Other aspects of local government policy provided the left with opportunities to limit Thatcherism. The handling of the legislation to impose rate capping, and the difficulties in enforcing it, showed the extent of the local government crisis. The government's reluctance to embark upon rate capping was conceded by Local Government minister, Lord Bellwin, in April 1984. As he told the Lords, the government deeply regretted the necessity for the proposed measures which should not have been needed. In its manifesto, the government had promised to act, and the Bill was the result. He supported the measures reluctantly, but unequivocably and wholeheartedly.

It had been forced on the government by a continual upward trend in local government expenditure, despite four years of trying to limit it through the traditional approaches of exhortation and local democratic accountability. Year after year, spending plans had to be revised upwards to allow for overspending. The overspend for 1984–5 was in excess of £850 million, of which 75 per cent was accounted for by fewer than twenty authorities. The emergence of hard left local authorities since 1979 had resulted in a rapid deterioration of the convention that local government would manage its affairs within broad guidelines established by central government and approved by parliament.[17]

Ultimately, although the government succeeded in banning from office and surcharging the most recalcitrant of the left's council rebels in Liverpool and Lambeth, fresh elections and the failure to combat politicisation showed that the government had won a battle, not the war. By 1986, rates abolition was being openly canvassed by Environment Secretary, Nicholas Ridley, following the Public Accounts Committee's critical report on local authority finance. The Committee argued that 1981 legislation to control the capital expenditure of local government had not only 'signally failed' to control such expenditure, but had also had 'adverse effects' on the performance of local authorities. The report noted the almost unlimited power enjoyed by local authorities to switch money allocated by government for one purpose to other uses and states: 'We fail to understand why the Government should continue to go to such lengths in the preparation of detailed spending programmes which it does not seek to have imple-mented'.[18] Thus one backbencher recalled that 'I do not like local government and have a high spending local authority. I like a cent-ralised unitary state as they have in France',[19] while another noted a typical lament that 'I disagreed over Rate Support Grant. I could not see why low spending authorities should bail out high spending Labour authorities'.[20]

By the time of the 1987 General Election, the abolition of the whole rating system and its replacement by a Community charge (or poll-tax to its opponents), was the adopted policy. The hope was that the new system would bring home to all citizens the real cost of local government service, leading to spendthrift councils being penalised at the ballot box. This reform was left for the third term and was a tacit admission of the government's failure to deal with local authority politically motivated over-spending in the 1979–87 period. The 1987 manifesto also promised to strengthen democratic processes in local government in the light of the Widdicombe Report, published in June 1986.

David Widdicombe, who chaired the inquiry, found that in-creased political polarisation was adversely affecting the quality of local democracy. The unanimous report suggested that local authority employees at the rank of principal officer and above should be barred from seeking election in neighbouring author-ities. To give minority parties more rights, the report urged the adoption of parliamentary-style question times and discussions of business chosen by minority councillors. Committees which could take decisions on behalf of the whole council should reflect the political makeup of the council, it said. It wanted a change in standing orders to require the public gallery to be cleared during disturbances. The report stated: 'We have been concerned to hear of disturbances at meetings of councils, especially in some London boroughs, and in some cases this appears to have amounted to intimidation. It is important that there should be no suspicion of connivance by the chair in such disturbances and accordingly, that there should be a duty on the chairman to bring them to a halt'.[21] It came out against co-opting non-councillors on to committees and wanted a further review of the role of teachers on education committees. The inquiry examined the chief executives' roles and urged that they should be given legal powers to ensure that council business was conducted fairly. After looking at various ways of electing councillors, it backed whole councils being re-elected every four years.

It may be argued that the government had not needed a report to describe what had been self-evident for some years, but the consideration of such micro-political reforms indicated an interest in tackling the left's sources of power rather than the consequences of that power. Thatcherism at local level needed Widdicombe-style changes to defeat the left rather than broad changes such as rate capping and structural re-organisation. Thus local authority over-manning, a major source of wasteful spending and high rates, was left untackled by the 1983–7 Government. Nicholas Ridley could only bemoan in October 1987 that local authorities had increased staffing levels for the eighth successive year to a record figure for both full-time and part-time staff of 2,491,607, an increase of 6,221 full-time and 36,677 part-time council workers in a year. That many new staff were examples of the left helping its own with political appointments showed the limits of Thatcherism. By 1987, local government was the last haven of the professional hard left able, not to defeat Thatcherism, but to deny its full potential in many parts of the country. It marked the left's most successful resistance to the Thatcherite assault on the post-war consensus and promised to continue to be so until government policy focused on specific abuses rather than on generalised targets.

In conclusion, the British left has survived the Thatcher period well. Despite three election defeats and its eviction from the corridors of power, the left has fought a semi-successful rearguard defensive action. The Labour Party has not been overtaken by the Alliance nor eliminated from its geographically based heartlands. To be sure, it has been defeated – but in the battles of 1979, 1983 and 1987, not in the war itself. At the end of eight years of Thatcherism, Conservative and Labour have never been further apart. There is no debate between them, no hint of a consensus. Deep divisions have always been a feature of Britain's class-oriented social structure. Class politics pre-dates Thatcherism, perhaps pre-dates the rise of the Labour Party. But embattled and irreconcilable political division has become an aspect of the post-1979 period, markedly so after privatisation gathered pace in the second term. In Britain, right and left are united only in rejecting the constitutional reformism of the Alliance. Economically and politically they inhabit different worlds. It seems light years ago that both parties were regarded by a cynical electorate, with much justification, as being basically the same. The British left cannot come to terms with Thatcherism without either the Labour Party renouncing socialism or the Alliance replacing Labour. Both options had closed by 1987. For Thatcherism to defeat the left it had to keep winning general elections.

CHAPTER 8

The Limits of Thatcherism and Intellectual Opinion

Thatcherism, with its stress on enterprise, business and wealth creation, has repeatedly clashed with informed, intellectual, or 'establishment' thinking. The Church of England bishops and many clergy, the Universities and school teachers, parts of the senior civil service and the BBC have all come into conflict – in some cases protracted and bitter – with Thatcherite concepts and policy initiatives. This uneasy and unsatisfactory relationship is not particularly surprising. Intellectual and opinion-forming thinking in the post-war era was centrist or centre-left in political direction. Thatcherism has attacked not only overt Socialism but consensus centre opinion.

Peter Riddell accurately observes that:

> For those outside the Conservative tribe, Thatcherism has appeared to be a bogey. The biggest shock has been for the centrist establishment – the world of senior civil servants, lawyers, top bankers, University lecturers and pundits. These have recoiled from the style as well as the content of Thatcherism, from its deliberate rejection of the consensus cherished by so many of them. Their doubts have been reinforced by Mrs. Thatcher's own evident dislike for the institutions in which many of them work – the Foreign Office, the BBC and the Bank of England.[1]

This is not to deny that all intellectual opinion is as resolutely hostile to Thatcherism, or to market led economic change, as was the case, for example, in the 1960s. There has been a shift in intellectual opinion, albeit slowly, towards Thatcherism and away from collectivism. Given the world-wide nature of the moves away from centralised, orthodox, state Socialism, it was to be expected that the socialist response to Thatcherism would be less intellectually penetrating than in an age when governments were perceived as capable of procuring steps, or strides, towards utopia. Thatcherism has shared in, and arguably inspired, the renaissance in individualistic, free-market thought which has occurred in many parts of the globe. In Britain, it is now the case that many more economists are sympathetic to the market than in the Keynesian heyday. More University economics and business studies departments in Universities and Polytechnics contain Thatcherites than was once the case. Classical liberalism has found its way back on political theory and philosophy student reading lists, in a reversal of 1960s social engineering and sociological fashion. And in the media and the civil service, supporters of the distinctly Thatcherite approach, as opposed to the consensus middle way, are identifiable, if hardly in profusion.

These intellectual developments in Britain are real and growing; but they are still outside, and alien to, the centrist intellectual opinion that still prevails. The Thatcherites are still a small intellectual minority with few voices – in a numerical rather than qualitative sense – in the BBC, higher education, and parts of the civil service. Like the Labour left, the centrist establishment has been able to limit Thatcherism but not to overwhelm or defeat it. Intellectually, although some Thatcherites claim otherwise, the movement of ideas which helped bring Mrs Thatcher to the Conservative leadership in 1975, has been outstripped in achievement by the extent of government policy radicalism. Thatcherism, where it has triumphed, has done so more by virtue of the government's political will than by the irresistible force of the New Right thinking. Britain's intellectual establishment has resisted with gusto. Indeed, intellectual hostility has often proved as strong as overt political opposition. Thatcherism is subjected to a continuous vilification. John Vincent has argued that:

> Inside Britain, Mrs. Thatcher is the object of an unthinking hatred not endured by any Prime Minister since the war, and perhaps not since Mr. Gladstone. We do not normally hate prime ministers. If Mrs. Thatcher is a cause of abnormal behaviour in others, the reason lies in the inability of progressive

orthodoxy, like any other orthodoxy, to tolerate earnest
and practical dissent. And Mrs. Thatcher's dissent is as earnest
as that of Cromwell and Gladstone. The hatred is infected with
snobbery. Mrs. Thatcher is the point at which all the snobberies
meet: intellectual snobbery, social snobbery, the snobbery of
Brooks's, the snobbery of Arts graduates about Scientists, the
snobbery of the metropolis about the provincial, of the South
about the North, and the snobbery of men about career
women.[2]

In the world of education the dispute between the professions and
the government has been fierce. School teachers have resented the
notion of payment by ability; opposed any reforms likely to
undermine their trade-union influence; used the strike weapon in
pursuit of pay claims; rejected the introduction of selectivity; and
opposed the publication of comparative examination performance
by different schools. To be sure, the small Professional Association of Teachers, which is broadly Thatcherite, is growing more
quickly than the other unions; but it remains small in total terms
and likely to remain so. More obvious market reforms have
engendered stiff opposition from the educational establishment.
The idea of education vouchers floated by Sir Keith Joseph as
Education Secretary was condemned by the teachers, fearful of
losing job security and hostile to competition. The DES officials
also helped to kill the voucher proposal. Arthur Seldon's study of
the political process which led the government to abandon its
voucher plans has revealed the depth of hostility within the
bureacracy to any reform which would weaken the permanent
officials' considerable powers.[3] Seldon pessimistically postulates
that the DES is so unlikely to favour vouchers that education
should be moved to 'an enterprise-oriented agency such as the
Manpower Services Commission'.[4] By the 1987 Election the
government was groping towards a form of simulated voucher (but
with another name), allowing greater parental choice and the
contracting out of LEA control. Payment for certain school
provision – trips out, concerts and so on – was raised by Kenneth
Baker.

In higher education, too, Thatcherite ideas were overwhelmingly
rejected by universities and dons. In a public display of disappro-
val, Oxford University in 1985 refused to award Mrs Thatcher an

honorary degree, hitherto an almost automatic award to a graduate who had become Prime Minister. By a 2:1 margin dons voted in congregation against the award, expressing a sentiment against 'cuts' and 'underfunding' that was widespread in University common rooms throughout the country. With a few exceptions, academics regarded taxpayer support, up to levels of 90 per cent or more, as a natural and desirable state of affairs. Many regarded universities not as satisfying customers (students) but as performing a task 'in the national interest' that had to be paid for as a priority from public expenditure. The conventional view was that government should finance universities but should not be concerned, on behalf of taxpayers, how the money was spent. This dream-world approach, of which the existence of academic tenure was the most obvious manifestation, made the nationalised industries prior to 1979 seem customer-oriented and enterprising by comparison. Many dons expected the 1960s expansion to continue unabated despite the growth in other claims on the public purse – more pensioners, more geriatric patients, the army of single-parent families, the expanding social security budget, and the costs of modernising Britain's armed forces.

The Thatcherite view that the universities could, and should, raise more of their own finance escaped the thinking of many dons. The added advantage that independence from state control gives higher education more freedom, fewer regulations and edicts from the Secretary of State, and greater academic variety, was rarely comprehended. The irony of the Oxford vote was that the University and its component but semi-autonomous colleges had flourished quite happily in the private sector since the 13th century. Only in 1919 did congregation vote by 126 to 88 to accept government funds. As in other universities, a small trickle of taxpayers' money developed into a flood over a fifty-year period, sapping University independence and downgrading the capacity to generate income from other sources. The hostility of University intellectual opinion towards the Thatcher Government can hardly be overstated. Although the government did not propose outright privatisation of any University – though strong arguments suggested that Oxford, Cambridge, Durham and Bristol, could quite adequately have joined Buckingham in a thriving private sector – the main thrust of government policy was to encourage University self-reliance. This approach amounted to privatisation by stealth, by encouraging each University to raise income from other sources.

By 1987, universities were consequently raising between 4 per cent (University of Ulster) and 23 per cent (University of Oxford) from sources such as sponsorship, endowments, investments, donations from alumni, market pricing of fees, conferences during vacations, expanding popular vocational subjects such as business studies and accountancy to cross-subsidise areas of scholarship, and overseas students. Reluctantly, and with a sullen resentment, universities were adjusting to Thatcherite market incentives while hoping that a Labour Government would rescue them with infusions of taxpayers' cash. Publicly they waged war against an uncaring government, cutting education with philistine insensitivity. The government was portrayed as harsh and anti-educational. Only one or two academics sympathetic to the removal of government money – and therefore government control – dissented.

Professor Ferns, Emeritus Professor at Birmingham University considered that:

> The harsh policy of the Government may prove a blessing in disguise. More than anything else, it has exposed the soft complacency of the universities in allowing themselves to become utterly dependent on the bounty of government. Some of us have long feared what has come to pass, and we are bound to say that what has proven inevitable is what the academic consensus has deserved.[5]

Similarly, Kenneth Minogue, Professor of Government at the LSE, considers the current state of the universities to be:

> an object lesson on the perils of dependence on the state. In the course of the twentieth century, universities have lost, step by step, the considerable autonomy they had previously enjoyed. They lost it because they were bribed into becoming functionaries of national policy. In the wake of the Robbins report, they were showered with gold, new universities were founded, jobs opened up and delightful prospects of power and importance unhinged the wits of simple academics. They unhinged more than just the dons. Students, in the best Gadarene tradition, could not resist the temptation of imitating the Marxists of

:ley and Paris. They rioted and protested in ways so
lent as to lose nearly all public sympathy. The result was to
universities both financially and politically helpless before
ext turn of Fortune's wheel.[6]

ese views are echoed by Professor Elie Kedourie, who has
:ated student loans rather than grants and suggested that the
·nment give the universities a capital endowment equivalent
: present discounted value of 10 or 15 years' grants, with each
ersity thenceforth liberated to fend for itself.[7] Such bold
ms were avoided by the 1983–7 Government. Moreover, it is
ely that the privatisation by stealth policy, which the govern-
was pursuing at the time of the 1987 Election, will bring swift
ge to the universities, where common room opinion is still
le enough to limit the intellectual acceptance of Thatcherite
et ideas to a small but growing number of dons who crave
)endence from all government control. Similar arguments
apply to state subsidy of the arts through the ubiquitous Arts
icil. Although former director of the Victoria and Albert
:um, Sir Roy Strong, has called for a return to private
)nage with 'the stimulation of the private sector not the
)ing of more money into the subsidised sector',[8] his voice is a
one. Most beneficiaries of state subsidy have bitterly attacked
government for underfunding. Moreover, the government
I be portrayed as philistine by suggesting that the arts should
more funds themselves. The 1983–7 Government, while
uraging a similar privatisation by stealth, as in the case of
:r education, did not abdicate completely from taxpayer
ort for the arts. Although powerful arguments exist[9] that the
vould flourish with less government funding rather than more,
overnment did not adopt the completely Thatcherite stance of
drawing all state subsidy even though that was the logic of its
y. Consequently, the arts lobby generally remained an articu-
niddle-class pressure group deeply hostile to market-oriented
:ing and committed to the notion that government financial
idence alone would benefit the arts. The view that the
ssive dominance of government – with the increase in lob-
5, committee meetings and political maneouvering – has held
artistic development in an unhealthy dependent way was very
1 a minority analysis. The arts lobby therefore contributed to

the intellectual opposition to Thatcherism by succeeding in keeping the end of government subsidy off the immediate political agenda. Another important source of intellectual informed opinion that clashed bitterly with Thatcherism in 1983–7, was the BBC. The first Thatcher Government had expressed dissatisfaction with the BBC's handling of aspects of the Falklands War, but most governments at some stage had criticised individual programmes allegedly displaying political bias. But in the second term a battle was joined on two separate fronts. Firstly, there was a marked intensification of allegations of left-wing bias which developed a high political profile under Norman Tebbit's chairmanship of the Conservative Party. Secondly, Thatcherite thinking on the extension of the concepts of the market and competition focused on the BBC's unique licensing system and duopoly position with ITV to dominate televised broadcasting to the disadvantage of customers and potential advertisers.

The left-wing bias claims, although a feature from time to time before 1983 – during the satire boom of the early 1960s, for example, – multiplied in the second Thatcher term. Firstly, there was the controversial *Panorama* programme, 'Maggie's Militant Tendency', shown on 30 January 1984, which suggested that four Conservative MPs had links with extreme right-wing racialist organisations. The *Daily Telegraph* described Conservative party reaction:

> Viewing of a recording at Conservative Central Office has produced a view among the party hierarchy that a number of those named are entitled to complain and could be justified in taking legal action.
>
> There is particular concern at the cutting of film to link flatly racialist occasions with material showing the party at work and the activities of the MPs named. One, it is said, apparently wears three different suits while addressing what is said to be the same meeting. Anyone who complains to the BBC or takes more serious action will have the backing of Mrs. Thatcher, who left little doubt yesterday that she shared the disgust felt by some senior colleagues over the programme – which she did not see.[10]

The then party Chairman, John Gummer, stated that the programme contained 'outrageous statements ... guilt by association and

McCarthyite comment'[11] and the MPs involved issued writs for libel. Following a meeting between Mr Gummer, the chief Whip John Wakeham and BBC executives, which failed to settle the dispute, the case inevitably ended in the law courts in October 1986. Under legal scrutiny, the BBC's arguments fell apart. The case was concluded in mid-trial when the BBC unreservedly withdrew allegations broadcast in the programme that two Conservative politicians were linked with extreme racialist Nazi and fascist organisations. The corporation agreed to a full apology, to be printed in *Radio Times* and to be broadcast in *Panorama*, in an out-of-court settlement of the libel suits brought by Mr Neil Hamilton, MP for Tatton, and Mr Gerald Howarth, MP for Cannock and Burntwood. Mr Hamilton and Mr Howarth received £20,000 in damages and legal costs of £240,735. The total cost to the BBC, including its own defence, was £500,000.

Both MPs said later that they had been fully vindicated and demanded that the BBC officials responsible be punished. 'The techniques employed by Panorama were worthy of Dr. Goebbels', they said in a statement. The BBC had already reached out-of-court settlements with two other MPs and the high cost to the licence payer was a further source of Conservative criticism.

One of the libelled MPs, Neil Hamilton, published his own personal account of the affair. In the immediate aftermath of the programme, he recounted that he (and the other MPs):

knew what people would be thinking: it must be true because *Panorama* is the BBC's flagship. The programme was done with the force of its reputation and the authority it carried. We had been tried and found guilty in absentia.

We suddenly found that speaking engagements and invitations to dinner were cancelled. We knew that there was no prospect of our being given a job in the government, not even as an unpaid parliamentary private secretary. Our families had to go out to see friends knowing what was in their minds. A number of veteran MPs advised us: 'You can't win against the BBC. People will forget about it sooner or later'. I spoke to friends in the legal profession and we went to see Peter Carter-Ruck, the solicitor who specialises in libel cases. He advised us to issue a writ for libel and that is what we did, within a week of the broadcast.

We had no idea that the case was going to be so l
remember when we got the first bill for legal fees, £875 e:
had just sold my house in Southsea and was waiting to l
house in my constituency, so I had some spare funds. If s
body had told us then that the bill at the end would run to
million pounds, we might never have gone through with i

The libel case, which took two and a half years to settle, poi:
relations between the BBC and the Conservative Party. T
libel was admitted by the BBC is a legal fact; but to
observers, the sloppy, unprofessional and personalised wa
programme had been made indicated that journalistic stan
had fallen considerably. A programme about 'Powellite' imn
tion views within the Conservative Party generally could cer'
have been made without grotesque smears against inn
individuals.

A second controversial programme which brought conflic
tween government and the BBC, concerned Northern Ire
long since a touchy subject for successive governments – in
too touchy, as the BBC had argued. Following the IRA's att
to assassinate Mrs Thatcher and members of the governme
Brighton in October 1984, any BBC programme screenir
interview with the IRA's chief of staff (or a senior member
hierarchy) was bound to generate intense controversy. St
programme was 'At the edge of the union', about extremi:
Northern Ireland, featuring both Catholic and Protestant para
tary leaders. Mrs Thatcher said that if the BBC were to go a
with any such programme, she would 'condemn them utterly
IRA is proscribed in Britain and in the Republic of Ireland
have lost between 2,000 and 2,500 people in the past 16 ye.
feel very strongly about it and so would many other people'

Earlier, Mrs Thatcher had called, in what became a l
quoted phrase, for terrorists to be starved of the 'oxyge
publicity'. Home Secretary, Leon Brittan, also made clea
opposition to the programme and, amid the political fall-ou
BBC governors banned the intended meeting. Michael Lea
has described the scene when the governors, under vice-chai
William Rees-Mogg's tutelage, viewed the offending film
follows:

As the coffee was being served, the film began to run on the five screens scattered round the room. It was clear, almost from the start, that the group, staring in almost total silence, did not like it. A sullen, disapproving mood prevailed, like an impossibly extended catching of the breath. Afterwards, Rees-Mogg and about half the governors went into a conclave near one of the screens. The management people thought that ominous. There were suggestions that someone should go and break up the circle. Nobody did.

After the viewing, the governors returned to the board room to reconvene in formal session. Rees-Mogg was invited by Young to speak first and did so in moderate terms, striking a keynote for the other governors. The programme was totally unacceptable and ought not to be shown.[14]

The government was now involved in a full-scale row over censorship which precipitated a protest strike by BBC journalists and technicians. Eventually, the programme was shown – the screening itself an anti-climax to the political conflict it had engendered.

Thirdly, the BBC clashed with the Conservative Party, and its Chairman Norman Tebbit in particular, over the coverage of the American bombing of Libya in April 1986. This row rumbled on for almost two years amid accusations of bias and their rebuttal by the BBC. A media monitoring unit was set up at Conservative Central Office to combat alleged bias, and it prepared a detailed dossier on the Libyan bombing coverage. Published in October 1986, the dossier accused the Corporation of inaccuracy, innuendo, imbalance and uncritical carriage of Libyan propaganda in its coverage of the US air strike against Tripoli in April 1986. It claimed that while ITN preserved an impartial editorial stance, the BBC 'took a number of editorial and journalistic decisions the effect of which was to enlist the sympathy of the audience for the Libyans and to antagonise them towards the Americans'. The BBC had stressed the 'worldwide condemnation' of the US action without supporting evidence, stressed the civilian casualties of the raid, giving emphasis to one of Libya's main propaganda points, and had gone into 'alarmist hyperbole' about the likely Libyan reaction. The individual reporting of BBC journalists was also criticised in the same manner. In an accompanying letter to the acting Chairman of the BBC board of Governors, Lord Barnett, Mr Tebbitt stated that:

> I enclose an analysis which Conservative Central Office has made of BBC TV's news coverage of the US raid on Libya in April of this year. It raises some very serious questions as to the way in which the BBC reports the news. For our analysis, we have taken as a yardstick the BBC's own public commitment to impartiality and balance. In the light of our evidence, you may feel that the BBC news reporting, in this instance at least, fell far short of the high standards which the corporation espouses. Indeed, you may conclude that far from being balanced, fair, and impartial, the coverage was a mixture of news, views, speculation, error and uncritical carriage of Libyan propaganda which does serious damage to the reputation of the BBC.[15]

The BBC responded with a detailed line-by-line rejection of Mr Tebbit's allegations, which in turn drew further criticisms of BBC evasion of the dossiers' contents. The controversy was bitter, personal and prolonged, adding to the antagonism occasioned by 'Maggie's Militant Tendency' and 'At the edge of the union'. Other allegations of bias also surfaced which were not so epic in terms of length. Conservative MPs criticised 'The Monocled Mutineer' drama about a mutiny by British troops in the First World War. The historical consultant employed by the BBC to advise on the production called it a 'tissue of lies' and 'riddled with errors'. That the drama had been written by Alan Bleasdale added to the criticisms of left-wing bias.

Another drama programme which was similarly attacked was 'Casualty'. The Conservative Central Office monitoring unit stated that there had been an 'enormous number' of complaints about 'Casualty', accusing it of obsession with health service cash cuts, understaffing, low pay and morale and hostility to the government's encouragement of contracted-out ancillary services. 'People think the programme is terribly biased – the characters come straight out with all the Labour Party criticisms of the way the health service is run'.[16] Health Minister Edwina Currie also castigated the programme for denigrating the way in which the Health Service operated. Similarly, it was alleged that the BBC were refusing to broadcast a play by Ian Curteis about the Falklands War because Mrs Thatcher was depicted in a favourable light. Godfrey Hodgson's book on the relationship between politicians and the BBC states that Mr Curteis claimed he was leaned on by BBC Head of Plays, Peter Goodchild. Hodgson described that:

> Afterwards, Ian Curteis argued, with mounting indignation, that the BBC didn't like his play purely because it painted Margaret Thatcher in too sympathetic a light. Goodchild, according to Curteis, was 'unhappy' at scenes showing Mrs Thatcher's private grief over casualties, and at the play's placing the Falklands War in the long tradition of British resistance to aggression. Again, according to Curteis, Goodchild also wanted him, among other things, to write in passages suggesting that military decisions in the War Cabinet had been influenced by electoral considerations. This, Curteis considered, was particular 'dynamite', as his play was carefully based on the historical record. He felt he was being asked to falsify that record.[17]

All these episodes left the impression that the government and the BBC were locked in a protracted political battle rather than occasionally clashing, as had been the case before 1983. Leon Brittan recalled that 'A lot of people in the BBC are anti-government, but it's not an organised thing – there wasn't a plot'.[18]

Although it can be pointed out that the Alliance criticised the BBC for not giving their spokesman sufficient air time, and Labour MPs perceived anti-strike bias, the main conflict was between the BBC and the Conservative Party over allegations of bias. By 1987, examples of bias were regularly being cited by Conservatives in a way that was quite different from the occasional controversy of the pre-Thatcher age. Whether or not the bias allegations were accurate is outside the scope of this study, but the fact remained that the BBC was an institution averse to Thatcherite influences and thus more likely to clash with Thatcherite opinion. This basic and fundamental conflict was exemplified by the BBC's resistance to government suggestions that it should take advertisements and re-structure its finances to reflect market forces.

The BBC's free-market critics were quick to point out that the corporation was funded by a regressive tax (the licence) resented and evaded by those on low incomes; was overn with powerful trade unions dominating management; was w in its use of resources; had long since abandoned its comm to public service, Reith-style, broadcasting in favour of game and soap operas; that downmarket programmes could easily advertising; that covert advertising existed in the form of l trailers for its own programmes and the sponsoring of te sporting fixtures; that an unhealthy duopoly existed with ITV could maximise its advertising revenue by charging above the ∎ price; and that consumer choice was more restricted than ir countries with a more market-oriented system.

Mrs Thatcher herself by 1984 was known to favour ▍ advertising on BBC. Not surprisingly, therefore, whe Peacock Inquiry into the BBC's future was announced in 1985, the question of replacing the licence fee with advertisi on its agenda. Public opinion polls moreover, showed a ▍ ment against the ever-rising TV licence fee and a preferenc per cent for pegging the fee and taking some advertising.[1] Brittan, the then Home Secretary, recalled that 'there growing concern about the licence fee and a growing fee favour of advertising though I was under no pressure Number 10. I knew Professor Peacock as a free market eco but he wasn't a slot machine. I deliberately phrased the te reference widely and thought it was an excellent report'. Peacock Inquiry took sixteen months to report, during wh acrimonious debate developed between those favourir Thatcherite market solution and those supporting the immunity from advertising – the BBC, ITV, the Labour (excluding mavericks such as MP Joe Ashton), the Allian much middle-class opinion, fearful of 'commercialisation BBC, while Peacock was sitting, even commissioned John to advertise between programmes on the excellence of the service, thus adding a touch of irony to the national d Professor Peacock himself often displayed a bemused baff at the controversy his inquiry was generating. Michael Le describes him in his history of the BBC as:

> anxious to allay the fears of the broadcasters that he wa mad axeman bent on chopping down all the trees in the

no matter how many years of vigorous life they still had in them. A Scot with a mild and persuasive accent, his moderate manner belied his awesome reputation and his intellectual rigour. He stressed that he and his committee – whose members included that other redoubtable Scot, Alastair Hetherington – had not been appointed simply to do the Government's bidding.

'I detect a touch of frenzy in the air', he said, 'as if my committee had the power of life or death over television. That is as far removed from reality as soap opera . . . Any suggestion that we are going to serve up a dish of pre-cooked political nostrums should be dismissed'. They were independent people and would judge the issues on their merits.[21]

The inquiry was told that advertising would threaten editorial independence of the BBC's National Union of Journalists' employees; that advertising would ruin programme schedules according to the BBC's then Chairman, Stuart Young; and that there would not be enough advertising to go round if the BBC broke ITV's monopoly. Alistair Milne, the BBC's Director General, told the inquiry that:

> The licence fee is a contract between broadcasters and the public. The public is arbiter and paymaster; we try in turn to give of our best and learn by so doing. And the more thoroughly we have looked at alternative ideas and suggestions for financing the BBC, the more convinced we have become that the public interest (not the BBC interest) is best served by the continuance of the licence fee as the most appropriate financial source of the BBC.[22]

Establishment and intellectual opinion was expertly mobilised to convince the Peacock Inquiry to back the status quo. As an example of pressure group lobbying, the BBC's performance was most impressive. Even though supporters of Thatcherite reform had strongly criticised the BBC's obsession with programmes such as *Dallas, Dynasty, Wogan,* and *Eastenders* – and the *Roland Rat* purchase from ITV – they found that it was they who were labelled 'philistine'. A market system, it was alleged, would lead to a lowering of standards – as if the BBC's output was not already extremely commercial.

When Peacock finally reported in July 1986, the BBC had effectively won the political battle. The Thatcherite option of scrapping or reducing the licence fee was not recommended and the BBC–ITV duopoly continued as before. The report looked to the distant future rather than the present, envisaging the day when by technological advance televisions could receive direct subscription services. Even the option of privatising Radios One and Two was not unanimously recommended. Not only was the licence fee system to be unreformed but a car radio licence (or tax) was proposed on top. Only four of its seven members backed a proposal to put up for auction all fifteen independent TV franchises when the contracts expired in 1988.

The first step on the road to a free-market system would be to adapt television sets for direct subscription, which in turn would replace the licence fee during stage two in the late 1990s. The final stage in the twenty-first century would introduce an era of 'electronic publishing', in which consumers would buy packages of programmes in much the way that they buy newspapers. A key provision was that the free-market should be supplemented by a subsidised public service network, administered by a new Broadcasting Council, to provide programmes of minority or specialist interest with the accent on 'knowledge, culture, criticism and experiment'.

Although it could be claimed that the ultimate thinking of the Peacock Report was Thatcherite to a certain extent and although the report was greeted as a radical one, the reality was different. The ending of the licence fee system could have been effected by the 1983–7 Government, had the committee not recommended its retention. If privatisation of nationalised industries had proceeded on lines suggested by Peacock then the process would have timidly been deferred to the 1990s. Privatisation of much of the BBC's blatantly commercial programmes had effectively been killed off, and with it the chance to resurrect a government-financed, genuinely public service broadcasting system, independent of the economically regressive television licence. The BBC had thus limited Thatcherism but had not intellectually killed off the arguments which gave rise to the Peacock Inquiry. Whether in the long-term the BBC–ITV duopoly will be able for ever to prevent broadcasting liberalisation remains to seen; but in the 1983–7 period, the limits of Thatcherism were demonstrated by the way in which radical market change was postponed.

As well as education and the media, the churches proved intellectual opponents of Thatcherism, capable of well orchestrated, though less sustained, political attack. The 'Faith in the City' report was condemned by the government as echoing Marxist nostrums. The Bishop of Durham openly sided with the miners during the 1984–5 strike. Other bishops joined those critics who saw the government as uncaring and unnecessarily dividing society. The Church of England had ceased to be the Tory Party at prayer; its political stance, in a collective sense, was centrist, or slightly centre-left, and consequently the cloister was as antagonistic to Thatcherism as the common room or broadcasting studio.

Thatcherism by 1987 had directly confronted centrist establishment thinking and most intellectuals found the new philosophy and policy implications too uncomfortable to accept. While in policy terms the post-war consensus had vanished, those who still hankered after it dominated Britain's intellectual elite. The 'chattering class' as Peter Jenkins has called them, could not overturn Thatcherism, but they could selectively limit it.

CHAPTER 9

The Limits of Thatcherism and Electoral Behaviour

The restoration of the Conservative fortunes after the abject performances in February and October 1974 has been one of the successes of Thatcherism in the context of electoral politics. Having lost four elections out of five between 1964 and 1974, the Conservatives have since won three consecutive victories. In doing so, a number of myths have been shattered; that high unemployment would lead to defeat in 1983; that right-wing Conservatism would be too divisive to win enough votes in the North to secure national victory; that Mrs Thatcher was too personally unpopular to win three consecutive elections; and that once the 'Falklands factor' faded, the Conservatives could not win. The extent of Thatcherism in electoral terms has therefore been demonstrated, seemingly entrenching the Tories as the 'natural party of government' they have always claimed to be.

But electoral limits have also been evident. The percentage share of the vote has been virtually static since 1979. In that first victory the Conservatives polled 44 per cent, in 1983 42 per cent, and in 1987 43 per cent. Thatcherism has therefore ruled in government on a national minority support, taking advantage of a split opposition and the vagaries of the first past the post electoral system. Electoral volatility, long recognised as a feature of British politics which emerged noticeably in the 1970s and 1980s, has also caused the Conservatives severe by-election and local government election embarrassment. In the 1983–7 parliament, faced with a collapse in public support, the Conservatives were by no means certain of re-election at the next general election. The volatility of electoral support caused considerable anxiety, which heightened the intra-party ideological tensions described in Chapter 6.

lections proved to be a series of humiliations. Between
in eight by-elections, the Conservative vote was down on
e by 14.1 per cent, contributing to the loss of Portsmouth
and Brecon and Radnor, where the Conservative candidate
poor third. In April 1986, Fulham was lost to Labour and
Derbyshire West was just held in May, Ryedale was
ed by the Liberals with a 4,940 majority, overturning a
vative majority of 16,142. The Conservatives were third at
Newcastle-under-Lyme, won by Labour, and Greenwich,
y the SDP, in July 1986 and February 1987 respectively.
the Conservatives' debacle at Brecon and Radnor, the last
he party had slumped from first to third was the 1958
ale by-election; moreover, their share of the vote had fallen
8 per cent to 28 per cent, equivalent to the falls in 1981 at
gton and Crosby. Although by-elections are a notorious
to general elections, this does not stop politicians from
ng in them either undue optimism (usually the Alliance) or
pessimism (usually the Conservatives). The Conservatives'
y-election results, up to and including Greenwich only four
s before the general election, contributed to the unease with
many in the party approached the campaign. While objec-
by-elections are psychologically different to the voters than
l elections, volatile results will continue to occur. Neverthe-
hey were a constant reminder of the vulnerability of the
erite appeal, especially mid-term. One MP, who was option the party's electoral prospects recalled that 'I showed my
uency party a chart of average popularity of governments.
ere on track and even a bit ahead had it not been for
nd. I had a bet with Nigel Lawson that the Alliance would
e Labour – he bet me it would not happen and was proved
[1] Another Thatcherite backbencher also argued that 'the
)P Alliance replacing Labour was a fear. Kinnock stopped a
switch to the Alliance which was a massive achievement
he has not got credit for. The destruction of Hatton was
nt – a superb job'.[2] By contrast, one Cabinet minister argued
ently that 'after Foot, the election of the housemaid's cat
have led to an improvement. The housemaid's cat had
proved to be a failure. Kinnock can't get off his one track –
very limited person with an enormous capacity for self-
on'.[3]

Local election results also embarrassed the government in the same way as by-elections. It may cynically be argued that most voters treat local elections as a referendum on the government of the day at Westminster, and that their significance is overplayed. So, to the politicians involved, it is natural that they should be treated as portents of future national trends. In 1984 the Conservatives lost Birmingham, considered their local government jewel in the crown, and witnessed a Labour revival even in parts of southern England. In 1985 the Conservatives lost control of nine counties, leaving them in overall control of only nine. The Alliance emerged to hold the balance of power in twenty counties, changing the political map of the English shires. As a result, Alliance politicians continually argued that a 'hung parliament' (or 'balanced parliament', as they preferred to describe it) was a likely outcome at the next election. Interminable academic and television debate delved into the constitutional implications of such a development, including the possibility of a series of consecutive hung parliaments. Both Mrs Thatcher and Mr Kinnock were questioned at length about possible coalitions, which they both, sensibly, rejected. In the 1986 local elections Labour and the Alliance made widespread gains at the Conservatives' expense. Only in 1987, in the run up to the general election, did local results augur well for the Conservatives. Overall, local election results showed the unpopularity of the Thatcher government for large periods of the 1983–7 parliament. Moreover, Labour's local government successes further entrenched the left's town hall opposition to Thatcherism.

Opinion polls generally also told the same story of government unpopularity. From the end of the miners' strike in March 1985 to the end of 1986, Labour was ahead of the Conservatives – by 12 per cent at the height of the Westland affair. David Butler commented, at a time when Labour was ahead in the polls in March 1986, that 'Over the coming months, psephological uncertainty will persist. Mrs Thatcher needs a new Falklands factor, and the economic recovery by itself will have to be spectacular to offset the simplest, most compelling election cry – "Time for change" sounded premature in 1983 but could have a strong appeal by 1987'.[4] One wet backbencher however thought that 'I never seriously thought the Labour party would win as the significant issue would be the economy. It cannot be denied that reducing taxation was popular and holding firm on inflation put the economy into good shape. By 1986 we were drawing favourable comparison with America'.[5] And a junior minister on the left of the party noted that 'Something happened in the Summer of '86. There were the first stirrings of rising prosperity, complaints about unemployment disappeared'.[6]

In August 1986, a MORI poll put Labour still nine points ahead of the Conservatives, 41 per cent to 32 per cent, with the Alliance on 25 per cent, but by November 1986, MORI discerned a 40 per cent to 39 per cent Conservative lead over Labour, following the party conferences, and into 1987 the Conservatives' opinion poll fortunes were boosted by the budget, Mrs Thatcher's visit to Moscow, Labour's renewed internal squabbles over black sections and falling unemployment. The Observer/Harris poll on 26 April 1987 gave the Conservatives an 11 per cent lead, 42 per cent to 31 per cent over Labour and similar leads promoted Mrs Thatcher's decision to call, on 11 May, a general election for 11 June. Reviewing the run-up to the election, one senior Conservative party official, recalled that 'Our conference turned the polls round. It was organised rather than stage managed. For the first time, all the speeches had a theme and special advisers helped to write them. The speeches were ready on time for press releases. The manifesto was delayed as well as policy decisions because Mrs Thatcher didn't want to commit herself to a June election. A lot of things were left to the last moment'.[7] Despite difficulties during the campaign, the Conservatives started off full of confidence with a radical manifesto. As one backbench MP put it 'the 1983 manifesto was bland but 1987 had several radical elements, some of which enlisted the support of the former wets'.[8] Table 9.1 indicates that the Conservatives held a consistent lead over Labour during the campaign.

But despite the Conservatives' steady lead, their campaign suffered some difficulties according to Rodney Tyler's book *Campaign*.[9] Allegedly, Lord Young had to intervene in the campaign to usurp Norman Tebbit's role as Party Chairman by instigating a change in advertising strategy. After the election, an undignified conflict over exactly what happened was made public. One senior party official, who totally rejects the Tyler account, recalled that 'the campaign went according to plan, in every respect bar one – Mrs Thatcher's tours were a balls-up. Seven or eight people were in charge of them and bad feeling was engendered by the press

TABLE 9.1   The Poll of Polls
JUNE 1987 GENERAL ELECTION CAMPAIGN VOTING TRENDS

Dates	Fieldwork Sampling	Company (Publication)	C %	Lab %	Aln %	Other %	Total %	C-L %	C/Lab swing %
6–11.5	1,735(180)	NOP (Standard)	46	28	25	1	100	+18	−1
7–11.5	1,085(110)	GALLUP (Telegraph)	39	28	30	3	100	+11	+2.5
8–12.5	1,445(103)	MARPLAN (Guardian)	43	29	25	3	100	+14	+1
8–12.5	1,934(178)	MORI (Sunday Times)	44	31	23	2	100	+13	+1.5
11–13.5	1,424(73)	MORI (Times) (Adj)	43	32	23	2	100	+11	+2.5
11–14.5	1,521(65)	MORI (S/T) (Pnl)	44	30	25	1	100	+14	+1
13.5	1,020(50)	MARPLAN (D. Express)	41	30	26	3	100	+11	+2.5
13–15.5	1,040(97)	HARRIS (Observer)	42	33	23	2	100	+9	+3.5
13–15.5	3,164(100)	HARRIS (W/W) (Adj)	40	34	25	1	100	+6	+5
14–17.5	2,410(60)	NEWSNIGHT (Adj)	40	34	24	2	100	+6	+5
16–17.5	1,058(97)	HARRIS (TV-AM)	42	32	24	2	100	+10	+3
18.5	1,072(54)	MARPLAN (Today)	41	33	24	2	100	+8	+4
19.5	1,976(52)	NOP (I'dent) (Adj)	42	34	23	1	100	+8	+4
19–20.5	2,640(197)	GALLUP (Telegraph)	42	33	23	2	100	+9	+3.5
18–21.5	1,079(98)	HARRIS (TV-AM)	43	36	20	1	100	+7	+4.5
20–21.5	1,328(65)	MORI (S/T) (Pnl)	44	31	24	1	100	+13	+1.5
20–21.5	1,066(97)	HARRIS (Observer)	41	34	22	3	100	+7	+4.5
21.5	1,517(103)	MARPLAN (Guardian)	41	33	21	5	100	+8	+4
20–22.5	1,432(140)	GALLUP (S'graph) (Pnl)	42	33	23	2	100	+9	+3.5
20–22.5	1,386(66)	HARRIS (W/W) (Adj)	42	35	22	1	100	+7	+4.5
22–25.5	1,075(98)	HARRIS (TV-AM)	42	37	21	0	100	+5	+5.5
26.5	1,035(69)	MARPLAN (Today)	42	35	20	3	100	+7	+4.5
26.5	1,978(52)	NOP (I'dent) (Adj)	42	35	21	2	100	+7	+4.5
26–27.5	2,506(194)	GALLUP (Telegraph)	44.5	36	18	1.5	100	+8.5	+3.8
27–28.5	1,188(65)	MORI (S/T) (Pnl)	44	32	23	1	100	+12	+2
27–28.5	1,072(98)	HARRIS (Observer)	41	37	21	1	100	+4	+6
27–29.5	1,296(66)	HARRIS (W/W) (Adj)	41	37	21		100		

28.5	1,553(103)	MARPLAN (G'dian)	44	32	21	3	100	+12	+2
27–29.5	1,271(140)	GALLUP (S'graph) (Adj)	41.5	34	22.5	2	100	+7.5	+4.3
29.5	1,302(50)	MARPLAN (S. E'ss) (Adj)	45	31	23	1	100	+14	+1
29–30.5	1,420(73)	MORI (Times) (Adj)	44	32	22	2	100	+12	+2
30.5–1.6	2,116(60)	NEWSNIGHT (Adj)	40	36	22	2	100	+4	+6
30.5–2.6	1,573(100)	HARRIS (TV-AM)	42	36	20	2	100	+6	+5
1.6	1,063(69)	MARPLAN (Today)	44	33	21	2	100	+11	+2.5
2.6	1,989(52)	NOP (I'dent) (Adj)	43	34	20	3	100	+9	+3.5
2–3.6	2,553(200)	GALLUP (Telegraph)	40.5	36.5	21.5	1.5	100	+4	+6
3–4.6	1,305(65)	MORI (S/T) (Adj)	43	32	24	1	100	+11	+2.5
3–4.6	1,087(98)	HARRIS (Observer)	44	33	21	2	100	+11	+2.5
4.6	1,576(103)	MARPLAN (Guardian)	44	34	20	2	100	+10	+3
3–5.6	1,100(60)	HARRIS (W/W) (Adj)	40	35	24	1	100	+5	+5.5
3–5.6	1,275(145)	GALLUP (S'graph) (Pnl)	41.5	34.5	22.5	1.5	100	+7	+4.5
3–6.6	2,102(98)	HARRIS (TV-AM)	43	33	22	2	100	+10	+3
5.6	1,300(23)	MARPLAN (S. E'ss) (Adj)	47	30	21	2	100	+17	–0.5
5.6	1,065(69)	MARPLAN (Today)	43	35	21	1	100	+8	+4
5–6.6	1,443(73)	MORI (Times) (Adj)	43	34	21	2	100	+9	+3.5
8.6	1,575(103)	MARPLAN (Guardian)	45	32	21	2	100	+13	+1.5
8–9.6	2,122(99)	HARRIS (TV/AM)	42	35	21	2	100	+7	+4.5
8–9.6	2,005(195)	GALLUP (Telegraph)	41	34	23.5	1.5	100	+7	+4.5
9.6	1,086(69)	MARPLAN (Today)	43	35	21	1	100	+8	+4
9.6	1,702*	ASL (The Sun)	43	34	21	2	100	+9	+3.5
9–10.6	1,668(165)	MORI (Times)	44	32	22	2	100	+12	+2
10.6	1,633(103)	MARPLAN (Guardian)	42	35	21	2	100	+7	+4.5
10.6	1,668(52)	NOP (I'dent) (Adj)	42	35	21	2	100	+7	+4.5
June 11		**Final Result**	**43**	**32**	**23**	**2**	**100**	**+11**	**+2.5**

Abbreviations: 'Adj' indicates a marginals poll adjusted to reflect the whole country; 'Pnl' indicates a panel survey; W/W – Weekend World; I'dent – The Independent; S/T – Sunday Times; S'graph – Sunday Telegraph; S. Ex'ss – Sunday Express; ASL – Audience Selection Ltd; * – Telephone poll.   11.5 Thatcher announces election date

Source: The Times Guide to the House of Commons 1987, p. 279.

which accompanied her'.[10] Similarly, one party whip believed that '*Campaign* had Lord Young's fingerprints all over it. It is absolute rubbish in my view. We had one black day at a press conference but opinion was solid'.[11] A different view is provided by one Cabinet minister close to events who confessed that 'It was the worst five weeks of my life. The book *Campaign* is accurate on events that occurred in and around Central Office and Downing Street but greater credit should go to people like Nigel Lawson and John MacGregor'.[12] The most likely explanation is that the electorate had little inkling of the behind the scenes dispute and opinion was not noticeably affected by marginal shifts in advertising techniques resulting from internal party cabals. Indeed, the solidity of opinion poll findings would indicate that the Conservative campaign was not rescued from crisis and defeat in the way that Tyler claims.

The campaign strategy debate aside, the Conservatives progressed to a convincing victory. The Conservative Party won the 1987 General Election with a majority of 101, gaining 43 per cent to Labour's 32 per cent and the Alliance 23 per cent. This was a victory beyond the hopes of most Conservatives, which demonstrated the electoral sustainability and resilience of Thatcherism. On election night, ITV predicted a Conservative majority of 65 initially, while the BBC speculated that Mrs Thatcher could be 17 short of a parliamentary majority. One former Cabinet minister thought that: 'I anticipated a majority of between 40 to 60. No one seriously thought the Conservatives were not going to win but I was surprised by the size of the majority. My concern was the Alliance. I could not believe that enough Conservatives would switch to Labour but I could see the Alliance threat and if that happened, the political landscape would change. I rather enjoyed the '87 campaign but I was not enormously impressed by the campaign centrally'.[13] Similarly, one backbench MP commented that 'Throughout the parliament I thought we would win the election. Defence and unilateralism was an achilles heel for Kinnock. I was not expecting the Alliance to collapse as it did and I expected a spurt for the Alliance in the campaign which never came. The dual leadership was stupid',[14] and another backbencher thought that 'The three crucial things were the general improvement in the economy, tax cuts and defence. On those issues people could see that government was on one side and the opposition parties on the other'.[15]

The key to the Conservatives' triumph lay in conspicuous

differences in regional swings – and within regions – which greatly reduced Labour's chances of winning Conservative seats in the South or Midlands. Moreover, in many marginals, the Conservatives' vote had held up particularly well. Labour made a net gain of seats of 20, the Conservatives a net loss of 21 but in all 47 seats changed hands. Given such a Conservative victory, why should the outcome suggest the limits of Thatcherism?

The answer lies in the static Conservative vote, in the party's failure in Scotland to win more than 10 seats, and in its relatively poor performance in parts of the North. The North–South divide was evident as it had been in previous elections, although the concept has been seriously abused by over-simplification. The Conservatives' traditional northern middle-class seats continued to return Conservative MPs in far greater numbers than traditional Labour seats in the South. Stephen Ingle has pointed out that in 1987, 'in the North of England, the Conservatives polled more votes (37%) than Labour managed over the country as a whole; indeed they polled only 5% fewer than Labour in the North'.[16] Similarly, Butler and Waller have noted that:

The biggest variations from the standard national pattern were regional. Labour fared very well in the Metropolitan areas of the North of England, especially Merseyside, in Wales and in Scotland, which was clearly a disaster area for the Conservatives as they lost over half of their 21 seats. The Conservatives resisted the movement to Labour in the Midlands and the South and actually made three net gains in London, where they now have 58 of the 84 seats. This table tells a clear story:

	C% +/-	Lab% +/-	All% +/-
London and rest of South	+1.2	+1.1	-2.0
Midlands	+0.9	+2.1	-2.7
North	-1.8	+5.4	-3.5
Wales	-1.5	+7.5	-5.3
Scotland	-4.4	+7.3	-5.3
Great Britain	-0.1	+3.0	-3.0

But these figures should not be taken as simple evidence of a North–South divide. The Conservatives held on notably in some Northern areas such as Bury, Bolton, and most strikingly,

Batley and Hyndburn, while their vote went down west of Bristol and Labour made gains in some areas in the South and Midlands, such as Oxford East, Norwich South, Leicester South and Leicester East. Even in London, Labour secured positive swings in some boroughs such as Lambeth, Camden and Islington.[17]

Butler and Waller suggest that such voting patterns may lie in housing tenure, with home-owners in North or South more likely to vote Conservative. While anecdotal evidence – and the view of many politicians and canvassers – strongly supports this view, it is not universally accepted. Heath, Jowell and Curtice only partially accept the home-ownership thesis, arguing that 'housing may be a source of material interests in the same way that class is, and the character of those interests may be very similar too'.[18] In turn, this view has been attacked by Ivor Crewe[19] and David Denver[20] who reject the belief that Labour's decline is the result of the shrinking working class alone, rather than its policy stance, and that of the Conservatives, on issues such as home-ownership.

To this writer, the sale of 1 million council houses to their tenants and the rise in home-ownership to 67 per cent of households (compared to only 64 per cent in the United States) has illustrated both the scope and limits of Thatcherism. On the other hand, it has enabled the Conservatives to prosper in areas of the country and in social classes that were lost to them in 1974. The non-home-owning working class would probably never have had the opportunity to own property – with all the status and dignity that implies – unless Thatcherism had triumphed and permitted council house sales. Labour's opposition to the policy in 1983 and reluctant acquiescence to it in 1987 compounded the votes the Conservatives gained. First-time house-owners who had bought property from their local council – directly because of Mrs Thatcher – have been converts to Conservative voting, in many cases for the first time. The Conservatives' success in many southern new town or council house constituencies is evidence of this trend. In 1987, it enabled the Conservatives to win Ipswich, Thurrock, Battersea and Walthamstow, as well as to increase their majorities in seats such as Basildon and Billericay.

But on the other hand, with 67 per cent home-ownership, the Conservative vote is stuck at 43 per cent. Almost a quarter of home-owners at least do not vote Conservative, despite the

Labour Party's traditional hostility to private-sector housing. Such voters are mainly middle-class public sector professionals who resent Thatcherism and embrace public provision. The intellectual, consensus, centrist, establishment described in Chapter 8 would not consider home-ownership a reason for voting Conservative, unlike the working-class voters liberated from permanent local authority tenantry. Housing thus displays contradictory messages for Thatcherism. The limits of Conservative voting are also evident if the massive mortgage interest tax relief, running at £4 billion per annum, is considered. Clearly, first-time home-owners who have not bought from the council have yet to recognise the political incentive to home-owners Mrs Thatcher's government has provided. Mortgage interest tax relief therefore probably brings the Conservatives fewer votes than its proponents claim. In short, the Conservatives can be disappointed that, with council house sales and generous mortgage interest tax relief, 24 per cent of home-owners at least voted in 1987 for opposition parties. Indeed, a MORI poll conducted during the 1987 Election found that only 50 per cent of home-owners intended to vote Conservative.

Similar arguments apply to the political effects of privatisation. Individual share holders have increased from 2 million in 1979 to 9.2 million in 1987, while the Conservative vote has fluctuated at general elections, 44 per cent, 42 per cent and 43 per cent. While undoubtedly many first-time share holders in newly privatised industries may have voted Conservative for the first time in 1987 from fear of a renationalising Labour government, the total electoral gain for the Conservatives was less than may have been expected, given the over-subscription of privatisation floatation. It may be argued – *à la* Heath *et al.* – that Conservative-inclined voters tend to buy privatised shares rather than Socialists. But even if this point is fully conceded, the Conservatives failed to reap any electoral benefits from privatisation commensurate to the political energy invested in it. Table 9.2 shows both the strengths and weaknesses of the Thatcherite electoral appeal.

Among socio-economic groups ABC1, the Conservatives polled only 54 per cent in 1987, suggesting a sizeable middle-class intellectual or establishment antipathy to Thatcherism. But the C2 and DE groups indicate growing Conservative support particularly among men. The DE group registers an average vote for the Conservatives of 30 per cent in 1987, despite the party's poor

TABLE 9.2   Voting patterns

	SOCIO-ECONOMIC GROUP (ABC 1) 43% of voters (+3% since June 1983)					
	Men			Women		
	1983	1987	Change	1983	1987	Change
Conservative	53%	53%	0%	56%	55%	−1%
Labour	17%	19%	+2%	15%	17%	+2%
Alliance	27%	26%	−1%	28%	26%	−2%
Other	3%	2%	−1%	1%	2%	+1%
Conservative lead	36%	34%		41%	38%	

Base: 3,725 and 3,917 of sample (23,396)

	SOCIO-ECONOMIC GROUP (C2) 27% of voters (−4% since June 1983)					
	Men			Women		
	1983	1987	Change	1983	1987	Change
Conservative	38%	41%	+3%	43%	40%	−3%
Labour	35%	36%	+1%	28%	35%	+7%
Alliance	25%	22%	−3%	27%	23%	−4%
Other	2%	1%	−1%	2%	2%	+0%
Conservative lead	3%	5%		15%	5%	

Base: 2,373 and 2,306 of sample (23,396)

	SOCIO-ECONOMIC GROUP (DE) 30% of voters (+1% since June 1983)					
	Men			Women		
	1983	1987	Change	1983	1987	Change
Conservative	30%	31%	+1%	35%	29%	−6%
Labour	44%	48%	+4%	38%	49%	+11%
Alliance	23%	19%	−4%	24%	20%	−4%
Other	3%	2%		−3%	−2%	−1%
Conservative lead	−14%	−17%		−3%	−20%	

Base: 2,504 and 2,838 of sample (23,396)

WORKING CLASS
57% OF VOTERS (−2% since June 1983)

	Owner Occupiers 66% (+7)			Council tenants 37% (−1)		
	1983	1987	Change	1983	1987	Change
Conservative	46%	44%	+2%	25%	21%	− 4%
Labour	25%	32%	+7%	49%	59%	−10%
Alliance	27%	23%	−4%	24%	18%	− 6%
Other	2%	1%	−1%	2%	2%	0%
Conservative lead	21%	12%		−24%	−38%	

Base: 5,310 and 3,561 of sample (23,396)

THATCHER'S CHILDREN (18–24)
14% of voters (+1% since June 1983)

	Men			Women		
	1983	1987	Change	1983	1987	Change
Conservative	42%	42%	0%	42%	31%	−11%
Labour	35%	37%	+0%	31%	42%	+11%
Alliance	20%	19%	−1%	25%	24%	− 1%
Other	3%	2%	−1%	2%	3%	+ 1%
Conservative lead	7%	5%		11%	11%	

Base: 1,309 and 1,193 of sample (23,396)

AGE GROUP (25–34)
19% of voters (+1% since June 1983)

	Men			Women		
	1983	1987	Change	1983	1987	Change
Conservative	37%	41%	+4%	42%	37%	−5%
Labour	34%	33%	−1%	25%	33%	+8%
Alliance	28%	24%	−4%	30%	27%	−3%
Other	1%	2%	+1%	3%	3%	0%
Conservative lead	3%	8%		17%	4%	

Base: 1,584 and 1,700 of sample (23,396)

TABLE 9.2   Voting patterns *(cont)*

| | AGE GROUP (34–54) 33% of voters (+1% since June 1983) | | | | | |
| | Men | | | Women | | |
	1983	1987	Change	1983	1987	Change
Conservative	42%	42%	0%	46%	47%	+1%
Labour	29%	32%	+3%	24%	27%	+3%
Alliance	27%	24%	−3%	28%	25%	−3%
Other	2%	2%	0%	2%	1%	−1%
Conservative lead 13%		10%		22%	20%	

Base: 2,798 and 3,087 of sample (23,396)

| | PENSIONERS (65+) 23% of voters (+2% since June 1983) | | | | | |
| | Men | | | Women | | |
	1983	1987	Change	1983	1987	Change
Conservative	50%	48%	−2%	51%	48%	−3%
Labour	25%	32%	+7%	25%	32%	+7%
Alliance	23%	19%	−4%	23%	19%	−4%
Other	2%	1%	−1%	1%	1%	0%
Conservative lead 25%		16%		26%	16%	

Base: 1,616 and 1,991 of sample (23,396)
Source: MORI poll, *The Times* 13 June 1987

showing in many inner city areas of traditional Labour support in
Wales, Scotland and northern England. This would suggest, as
Butler and Waller argued, not so much a north–south divide but a
division between 'the haves and the have nots, the rich and the poor
... an election of social and political bifurcation ... the most polar-
ised within living memory'.[21] The economic division between working class and claimant class is now manifested in voting behaviour.

Table 9.2 also indicates a massive fall in Conservative appeal
among women in the 18–24 age group, unmatched among men.
This may well reflect that the growing concern about social
services, education and the NHS are priority issues among women
rather than men, particularly as the pattern is similar among the
24–35 age range. The most striking evidence however, concerns

the 57 per cent of voters categorised as working class. Although owner-occupiers voted 44 per cent to 32 per cent in the Conservatives' favour, the trend since 1983 was away from the Conservatives. However, an average Conservative vote of 23 per cent among council tenants may be regarded as a high percentage, given the regional distribution of the vote in 1987.

In summary, although the general election was an impressive victory for the Conservatives, indicating the longevity of radical Thatcherism against its critics, a number of aspects of the outcome suggested definable electoral limits. Mrs Thatcher herself recognised one of them, the inner cities problem, on election night at her Central Office celebration. Subsequently, Conservatives in Scotland began an inquest on the party's worse than expected performances. Former Scottish Secretary, George Younger, whose own Ayr seat was almost lost to Labour, recalled that:

Scotland was a massive protest vote. They were told Mrs Thatcher would win anyway and that the English would re-elect her. It was like a series of by-elections with tactical voting. Where we held on – Stirling and Edinburgh West for example – it was not clear which party would mount the challenge. I think there was a strong element of protest in 1974 and 1987. But in 1987 the Scots voted against the Conservatives but not for other parties. Scots may vote SNP but oppose nationalist policies.[22]

Following the election inquest the moribund state of some northern city Conservative associations was also targeted for overhaul in sharpening the party's message. These specific lessons may well be learned for the next general election and, while the opposition vote is divided between Labour and a third party grouping capable of obtaining roughly 25 per cent of the popular vote, the Conservatives may be satisfied with their electoral appeal. But the continued opposition of the public-sector middle-class and the intellectual opinion formers, the hostility of the sizeable claimant class, the regional economic and political distortions, and the maverick Scottish vote, all indicate that Thatcherism needs more than 43 per cent of the popular vote to secure its long-term electoral prospects. Until the Conservatives can pass the 50 per cent mark, they must depend on factors outside their control. Electoral behaviour has demonstrated the scope of Thatcherism but it has also shown limits which Conservatives need to rectify, not ignore.

CHAPTER 10

Concluding Thoughts

Although conclusions about Thatcherism as an historical phenomenon may be premature while Mrs Thatcher is still in power, it is
possible to look at the 1983–7 administration in its political and
ideological context. Mrs Thatcher's own domination of government and impetus behind its policy direction was a salient feature.
The use of Cabinet committees to devolve power away from full
Cabinet; the appointment of permanent secretaries if not overtly
sympathetic then at least not hostile to Thatcherism; the constant
re-shuffles of Cabinet and junior ministers; the appeal to Conservative party grass roots opinion against internal critics; the use
of the Number 10 press office to 'create' favourable news;[1] the use
of *ad hoc* discussion groups where policy is made;[2] the importance
of the Number 10 policy unit in providing information and advice;
the institutional downgrading of the civil service;[3] and the near
total mastery of Prime Minister's Question Time as a weapon for
baiting the Labour Party, are all manifestations of the Thatcher
style of Prime Ministerial government. Without such techniques of
wielding power, Thatcherism in policy terms would have been
stunted and ineffectual.

Whether or not Prime Ministerial government is a good or bad
feature of current British politics is outside the scope of this study.
However, it is a fact that any radical government, to overcome
civil service inertia, pressure group lobbying or internal party dis-
sension, must be propelled by a strong leader at 10 Downing Street.
Thatcherism in 1983–7 was constantly propelled by Mrs Thatcher.
However, as Peter Jenkins has argued, Mrs Thatcher 'did not
transform the role of Prime Minister in any institutionalised
sense'.[4] Indeed, it may be further canvassed that any institutional
change would have been un-Thatcherite in that her revolution has
always been one of attitudes and policies as opposed to 1960s

notions of institutional (or constitutional) change. The debate on her Prime Ministerial style is by no means complete and the views of her Cabinet ministers diverge on the evidence and extent of her autocracy. Jim Prior, Francis Pym, Michael Heseltine and, latterly, John Biffen, have all criticised Mrs Thatcher's over-forceful and intolerant style of controlling rather than consulting Cabinet. But Patrick Jenkin, dismissed by Mrs Thatcher in 1985, disagrees. In his view 'Prime Ministerial government is a lot of nonsense. The idea that you could not voice your own opinions is not true. She took all opinions and Whitelaw made it clear to her when she was out voted. With the exception of Heseltine, all the other [dismissed] ministers wanted to be sacked'.[5] Similarly, other Cabinet ministers considered that '1983–7 was less and less acrimonious with few people out of step. She is not autocratic, she just argues her case very strongly. Cabinet is not really the forum for solving disputes except in extremis',[6] and 'She's no different from any other Prime Minister, as Crossman shows. It is true that she is strong and leads from the front'.[7] One senior minister thought that 'a government is as autocratic as the temper of the Cabinet allows it to be. She has strong views – she is not a Baldwin or Attlee figure – but she does not always prevail',[8] while a colleague confirmed that 'I have not a lot of time for Prior, Pym, Heseltine and Biffen. They never said their piece in Cabinet. Walker keeps his mouth shut in Cabinet but makes opaque speeches outside. It is nonsense to say she runs an autocratic Cabinet'.[9] This debate clearly raises questions as to Thatcherism's survival under another Conservative leader which can be settled only by whoever should emerge duly elected by the parliamentary party. Thatcherite successors were not in over-supply during the second term and the most canvassed successor, Norman Tebbit, appeared to have removed himself from future consideration by resigning his Cabinet seat after the 1987 Election. John Moore was suggested as a long-term contender, but Thatcher-ites essentially were not considering succession unless involuntarily forced by a Westland type crisis.

Given Mrs Thatcher's effective stranglehold on the Conserva-tive leadership and the levers of Prime Ministerial power, the policy implementations of the second administration were con-siderable. Thatcherism in scope is a relentless and determined pursuit of ideological goals. Most were attained in 1983–7. Privat-isation was intensified from its humble and modest beginnings in

The Limits of Thatcherism

1979–83. Trade-union power was more effectively curbed by Arthur Scargill's defeat in 1985 than by any other single action. The trade-union veto on an enterprise economy was removed, publicly and painfully. Nationalised industry management, including competitive investment for profit, would never be the same again once Scargillism, as a political ideology, was tamed. The 1984–5 miners' strike was the single most important event in the course of the parliament to further Thatcherism. Economic policy could consequently maintain the stress on low inflation, sound budgetary control to reduce government borrowing, and ultimately cuts in taxation. Abroad, Thatcherism combined a basic nationalism with the status of the Prime Minister as the Western World's senior statesman, capable of 'doing business' with Mr Gorbachev, while stressing multilateral disarmament to maximum domestic political advantage.

The scope of Thatcherism, in policy and electoral terms, outweighed the limits but did not remove them. Thatcherism, noted Butler and Waller, 'has not as yet won undivided or even consistent support amongst the citizens of the United Kingdom, even in the hour of ... unprecedented triumph'.[10] Electoral limits reflected the intense hostility Thatcherism had encountered from certain social groups who fought rearguard actions against it in local government, the BBC, parts of the media, the schools, universities, and the churches. Thatcherism had defeated but not destroyed the Labour left and Alliance centre. Within the Conservative Party, the dissidents over economic policy also considered their cause worth fighting for. But the composition of the parliamentary Conservative Party is now more amenable to Thatcherism as it more accurately reflects the economic concerns of the population. As one whip accurately put it 'The parliamentary party has changed as we are getting fewer old style gentry and gifted amateurs. We are getting more people with a local government background and a more political intake. The party is bringing into parliament people who have had to worry about the mortgage and the electricity bill'.[11]

For all its policy successes, within the terms of its own ideology, including massive economic and industrial changes away from collectivism and in favour of market-oriented enterprise, Thatcherism and the Thatcherites ended their second administration with a renewed mandate but without a new national consensus. The post-war consensus based on nationalisation, Keynesianism, trade-union power and collective social provision had been largely overturned; but Thatcherism had not become a new consensus which would survive an uncertain future of continued political antagonism and electoral volatility. It was a measure of the scope and success of Thatcherism that it had got so far, but a measure of limits that it had so much more to do.

Notes and References

INTRODUCTION

1. M. Holmes, *Political Pressure and Economic Policy: British Government, 1970–4* (London: Butterworth, 1982).
2. M. Holmes, *The Labour Government, 1974–9: political aims and economic reality* (London: Macmillan, 1985).
3. M. Holmes, *The First Thatcher Government, 1979–83: contemporary conservatism and economic change* (Brighton: Wheatsheaf, 1985).

CHAPTER 1

1. P. Riddell, *The Thatcher Government* (London: Martin Robertson, 1983), p. 7.
2. P. Jenkins, *Mrs Thatcher's Revolution: the ending of the socialist era* (London: Johnathan Cape, 1987), p. 168
3. D. Kavanagh, *Thatcherism and British politics: The end of consensus?* (Oxford: OUP, 1987), p. 10.
4. *Guardian* (21 September 1987).
5. J. Cole, *The Thatcher Years: a decade of revolution in British politics* (London: BBC, 1987), pp. 8–11.
6. J. Gould and D. Anderson, 'Thatcherism and British Society', in *Thatcherism: personality and politics*, ed. Kenneth Minogue and Michael Biddiss (London: Macmillan 1987), pp. 46–9.
7. J. Gould and D. Anderson, 'Thatcherism and British Society', in *Thatcherism: personality and politics*, ed. Kenneth Minogue and Michael Biddiss (London: Macmillan 1987), pp. 46–7.
8. K. Minogue, *Thatcherism: personality and politics* (London: Macmillan 1987), p. 17.
9. S. Finer, *Thatcherism: personality and politics* (London: Macmillan 1987), pp. 128–9
10. D. Howell, *Blind Victory* (London: Hamish Hamilton, 1986).
11. J. Prior, *A Balance of Power* (London: Hamish Hamilton, 1986), p. 260.
12. F. Pym, *The Politics of Consent* (London: Sphere, 1985), pp. 18–19.
13. R. Tyler, *Campaign: the selling of the Prime Minister* (London: Grafton Books, 1987), p. 251.
14. *Morning Star* (28 March 1984).

15. R. Levitas, *The Ideology of the New Right* (London: Polity 1986), S. Hall and M. Jacques (eds), *The Politics of Thatcherism* (Edinburgh: Lawrence & Wishart 1983). See also *Marxism Today*, passim.
16. M. Jacques, *Guardian* (14 December 1987).
17. T. Dalyell, *Thatcher: Pattern of Deceit* (London: Cecil Woolf, 1987).
18. A. Walters, *Britain's Economic Renaissance* (Oxford: OUP, 1986) pp. 94–5.
19. Kavanagh, *Thatcherism*, pp. 299–300.
20. P. Hain, *Political Strike: the state and trade unionism in Britain* (Harmondsworth: Penguin Books, 1986), pp. 94–5.
21. Kavanagh, *Thatcherism*, p. 34.
22. Jenkins, *Mrs Thatcher's Revolution*.
23. John Vincent, 'Margaret Thatcher: her place in history', *Contemporary Record*, 1 (3) (1987), pp. 23–4.
24. For a full account of the Heath U-turns see M. Holmes, *Political Pressure and Economic Policy: British Government, 1970–4* (London: Butterworth, 1982).
25. P. Hain, *Political Strikes*.
26. A. Roth, *Heath and the Heathmen* (London: RKP, 1972), p. xv.
27. For a fascinating insight into this period, see Sir D. MacDougall, *Don and Mandarin* (London: John Murray, 1987) Chapters 7–9.
28. J. Barnett *Inside the Treasury* (London: André Deutsch, 1982) especially Chapters 3 and 4.

CHAPTER 2

1. Interview, Cabinet minister.
2. Interview, M. Brown.
3. Interview, R. Needham.
4. BBC radio interview (11 September 1983).
5. White Paper, Cmnd 8789 (London: HMSO).
6. White Paper, Cmnd 9143 (London: HMSO).
7. Interview, Cabinet minister.
8. *The Times* (14 March 1984).
9. P. Browning, *The Treasury and Economic Policy, 1964–85* (London: Longman, 1986) p. 184.
10. Interview, junior minister.
11. *The Times* (20 March 1985).
12. G. Thompson, *The Conservatives' Economic Policy* (London: Croom Helm, 1986) p. 219.
13. *Sunday Telegraph* (7 July 1985).
14. Interview, L. Brittan.
15. R. Disney, in P. Cockle (ed.), *Public Expenditure Policy 1984–5* (London: Macmillan, 1984) p. 151.
16. Interview, Cabinet minister.

17. Interview, L. Brittan.
18. Interview, minister DHSS.
19. *The Times* (14 February 1986).
20. Interview, A. Burt.
21. Thompson, *The Conservatives' Economic Policy*, p. 214.
22. *The Times* (17 March 1987).
23. Interview, Teddy Taylor.
24. See R. Body, *Agriculture: the triumph and the shame* (London: Temple Smith, 1982) and *Farming in the Clouds* (London: Temple Smith, 1984).
25. HM Treasury, *Economic Progress Report* (September–October 1986).
26. See R. Howarth, *Farming for Farmers?* (London: IEA, 1985).
27. J. MacInnes, *Thatcherism at Work* (London: Open University Press, 1987), p. 57.
28. See M. Holmes, *The First Thatcher Government, 1979–83; contemporary conservatism and economic change* (Brighton: Wheatsheaf, 1985) Chapter 4.
29. S. Brittan, in *Monetarism and Macro Economics* (London: IEA, 1987) p. 122.
30. *The Times* (23 May 1986).
31. Interview, Lord Young.

CHAPTER 3

1. *The Times* (12 July 1983).
2. F. Chapple, *Sparks Fly* (London: Michael Joseph, 1984) p. 207.
3. *The Times* (1 August 1986).
4. P. Bassett, *Strike Free: new industrial relations in Britain* (London: Macmillan, 1987) p. 10.
5. Speech at IOD conference (25 February 1986).
6. Conservative Manifesto 1987.
7. M. Beenstock and P. Minford, in *Monetarism and Macro-Economics* (London: IEA, 1987) p. 135.
8. *Daily Telegraph* (31 January 1984).
9. *The Times* (8 January 1984).
10. Bassett, *Strike Free*, p. 60.
11. P. Hain, *Political Strikes: the state and trade unionism in Britain* (Harmondsworth: Penguin Books, 1986) p. 239.
12. Interview, P. Lilley.
13. Interview, Lord Jenkin.
14. See N. Hagger, *Scargill the Stalinist?* (London: Oak Tree Books, 1984) for a comprehensive collection of Mr Scargill's political philosophy.
15. *New Left Review* (July–August 1975).
16. Interview, G. Younger.
17. Interview, senior Cabinet minister.

18. M. Crick, *Scargill and the Miners* (Harmondsworth: Penguin, 1985) p. 99.
19. Interview, P. Walker.
20. I. Macgregor, *The Enemies Within* (London: Collins, 1986) p. 164.
21. For such an account see *Strike* by the *Sunday Times* Insight Team (London: Coronet Books, 1985).
22. *The Times* (1 June 1984).
23. BBC radio interview (19 September 1984).
24. Interview, Peter Walker.
25. *The Times* (6 November 1984).
26. Interview, L. Brittan.
27. Macgregor, *The Enemies Within*, pp. 188, 211, 236, 273–4, 336.
28. P. Jenkins *Mrs Thatcher's Revolution: The ending of the socialist era* (London: Jonathan Cape, 1987) p. 230.
29. Macgregor, *The Enemies Within*, p. 304.
30. Interview, senior Cabinet minister.
31. Interview, Cabinet committee member.
32. Interview, G. Gardiner.
33. Macgregor, *The Enemies Within*, p. 337.
34. *Sunday Times* Insight Team, *Strike*, pp. 216–24.
35. *Sunday Times* Insight Team, *Strike*, p. 216.
36. Interview, N. Tebbit.
37. Interview, N., Ridley.
38. Interview, R. Needham.
39. *Sunday Times* Insight Team, *Strike*, p. 100.
40. Interview, R. Needham.
41. Interview, Cabinet minister.
42. Interview, senior Cabinet minister.
43. Interview, L. Brittan.
44. Interview, Treasury minister.
45. Interview, M. Brown.
46. J. MacInnes *Thatcherism at Work* (London: The Open University Press, 1987) pp. 106–7.
47. Bassett, *Strike Free*, pp. 123–6.
48. Bassett, *Strike Free*, pp. 96–7.
49. Bassett, *Strike Free*, p. 2.
50. Barnett, *Strike Free*, p. 88.

CHAPTER 4

1. See M. Holmes, *The First Thatcher Government, 1979–83: contemporary conservatism and economic change* (Brighton: Wheatsheaf, 1985) pp. 8–10.
2. *The Times* (21 December 1984).
3. Interview, G. Gardiner.
4. Interview, R. Needham.
5. *The Times* (17 August 1983).
6. C. Veljanovski, *Selling the State* (London: Weidenfeld & Nicolson,

1987), and J. Kay *et al. Privatisation and Regulation – the UK experience* (Oxford: OUP, 1986).
7. *The Times* (2 November 1986).
8. Treasury consultative document on nationalised industries (1984).
9. K. Dowd, *Economic affairs*, 7 (3) (1987) p. 26.
10. M. Heseltine *Where There's a Will* (London: Hutchinson, 1987) p. 65.
11. *Sunday Times* (28 November 1984).
12. S. Finer, in *Thatcherism: personality and politics*, ed. Kenneth Minogue and Michael Biddiss (London: Macmillan, 1987) p. 131.
13. Interview, P. Walker.
14. Kay *et al. Privatisation*, p. 258.
15. G. Thompson, *The Conservative's Economic Policy* (London: Croom Helm, 1986) p. 201.
16. Quoted in Kay *et al., Privatisation*, p. 85.
17. C. Veljonovski, *Economic Affairs*, 7 (3) (1987) p. 21.
18. *The Times* (13 December 1983).
19. *The Times* (12 September 1986).
20. M. Edwardes, *Back from the Brink* (London: Pan 1983) p. 233.
21. *The Times* (5 February 1986).
22. Interview, Cabinet minister.
23. Interview, M. Brown.
24. Interview, R. Needham.
25. P. Jenkins, *Mrs. Thatchers's Revolution: the ending of the socialist era* (London: Jonathan Cape, 1987), p. 176.
26. Interview, Cabinet minister.
27. L. Copeland, *Economic Affairs*, 6 (6) (1986), p. 15.
28. D. Kavanagh, *Thatcherism and British Politics: The end of Consensus?* (Oxford: OUP, 1987) p. 221.
29. See particularly a report of Dr Owen's speech favouring privatisation, *Independent* (25 September 1987).

CHAPTER 5

1. Interview, C. Townsend.
2. D. Kavanagh, *Thatcherism and British Politics: The end of Consensus?* (Oxford: OUP, 1987) pp. 269–70.
3. P. Riddell, *The Thatcher Government* (London: Martin Robertson, 1983) p. 207.
4. Interview, former Foreign Office Minister.
5. BBC Interview (24 September 1987).
6. J. E. Powell, *The Common Market: the case against* (London: Elliott, 1971).
7. R. Cottrell, *The Sacred Cow: the folly of Europe's food mountains* (London: Grafton Books, 1987).
8. Interview, former Foreign Office minister.
9. Cottrell, *The Sacred Cow*, p. 13.

10. D. Elles in *Thatcherism* ed. Kenneth Minogue and Michael Biddiss (London: Macmillan, 1987) p. 101.
11. P. Jenkins, *Mrs Thatcher's Revolution: the ending of the socialist era* (London: Jonathan Cape, 1987) p. 287.
12. Ali M. El-Agraa, 'Mrs Thatcher's European Community Policy', in D. S. Bell (ed.), *The Conservative Government 1979–84* (London: Croom Helm, 1985), p. 182.
13. *The Times* (20 June 1983).
14. *The Times* (7 December 1983).
15. *The Times* (13 February 1984).
16. John Ardagh, 'Europe's Soured Ideal', *Sunday Times* (25 March 1984).
17. Elles, in *Thatcherism*, ed. Minogue and Biddiss, p. 102.
18. *Sunday Times* (23 December 1986).
19. Interview, T. Taylor.
20. Interview, P. Lilley.
21. *The Times* (25 November 1986).
22. Interview, T. Taylor.
23. Interview, European Reform Group member.
24. Conservative Manifesto 1987, p. 41.
25. See Cottrell, *The Sacred Cow*, Chapters 9–12.
26. This article was to have appeared in J. Bayliss (ed.), *Alternative Approaches to British Defence Policy* (London: Macmillan, 1983).
27. Conservative Manifesto 1983.
28. *The Times* (9 October 1986).
29. Speech to Conservative conference (10 October 1986).
30. *Independent* (13 June 1987).
31. Labour Party Manifesto 1983.
32. Alliance Manifesto 1984.
33. MORI poll in the *Sunday Times* (4 Janury 1987).
34. See J. E. Alt, *The Politics of Economic Decline* (Oxford: OUP, 1979) pp. 195–9.
35. Interview, G. Younger.
36. Interview, Conservative Whip.
37. R. Pfaltzgraff and J. Davis, in *British Security Policy and The Atlantic Alliance* (Oxford: Pergamon Brassey, 1987) p. 125.
38. Interview, Backbench MP.
39. Jenkins, *Mrs Thatcher's Revolution*, pp. 300–1.
40. G. Frost, in *British Security Policy and the Atlantic Alliance: prospects for the 1990's* (Oxford: Pergamon, 1987) p. 31.
41. Interview, C. Townsend.

CHAPTER 6

1. See M. Holmes, *Political Pressure and Economic Policy: British Government, 1970–4* (London: Butterworth, 1982), N. Wapshott and G. Brock, *Thatcher* (London: Futura, 1983) and R. Lewis, *Margaret Thatcher* (London: RKP, 1983 edn).

2. Interview, P. Lilley.
3. Interview, R. Needham.
4. Interview, A. Burt.
5. Interview, Treasury minister.
6. Interview, Sir B. Braine.
7. Speech to Foreign Exchange Dealers' Association (17 January 1984).
8. Interview, Conservative Whip.
9. *Sunday Express* (11 March 1984).
10. *The Times* (12 April 1984).
11. Interview, Lord Jenkin.
12. F. Pym, *The Politics of Consent* (London: Sphere, 1985), p. 9.
13. *The Times* (30 June 1986).
14. *The Times* (1 July 1983).
15. Interview, Conservative MP.
16. Interview, Conservative Whip.
17. Interview, Cabinet minister.
18. Interview, A. Burt.
19. Speech to Tory Reform Group, Brighton (11 October 1984).
20. J. Prior, *A Balance of Power*, (London: Hamish Hamilton, 1986) p. 253.
21. J. Cole, *The Thatcher Years: a decade of revolution in British Politics* (London: BBC, 1987) p. 165.
22. Interview, Conservative MP.
23. Interview, Cabinet minister.
24. Interview, Conservative PPS.
25. P. Hennessy, *Cabinet* (Oxford: Blackwell, 1986) p. 110.
26. Interview, Conservative Whip.
27. Interview, Backbench MP.
28. Interview, Michael Brown.
29. *The Times* (27 January 1986).
30. Interview, Sir B. Braine.
31. Interview, Cabinet minister.
32. Interview, Cabinet minister.
33. M. Heseltine, *Where There's a Will* (London: Hutchinson, 1987) p. 254.
34. J. Critchley, *Heseltine* (London: André Deutsch, 1987) p. 161.
35. Interview, R. Needham.
36. P. Jenkins, *Mrs Thatcher's Revolution: the ending of the socialist era* (London: Jonathan Cape, 1987) p. 213.
37. Interview, M. Brown.
38. *Sunday Times* (9 February 1986).
39. *Sunday Times* (18 May 1986).
40. Interview, G. Gardiner.
41. Interview, T. Taylor.
42. See R. Tyler, *Campaign: the selling of the Prime Minister* (London: Grafton Books, 1987) for a controversial account of the dispute between Mrs Thatcher and Mr Tebbit on this issue.

43.   D. Kavanagh, *Thatcherism and British politics: The end of Consensus?* (Oxford: OUP, 1987) pp. 278–9.
44.   Cole, *The Thatcher Years*, p. 201.
45.   P. Norton in *Thatcherism*, ed. Minogue and Biddiss, pp. 33–4.

CHAPTER 7

1.   According to a *Labour Party News* survey, reported in the *Guardian* (4 January 1988), Labour Party members are twice as likely to work in the public than the private sector, 7 out of 10 were home-owners and 60 per cent had a degree or diploma compared to 11 per cent of the population at large.
2.   B. Hindess, *The Decline of Working Class Politics* (London: MacGibbon & Kee, 1971).
3.   M. Crick, *The March of Militant* (London: Faber, 1986).
4.   R. Kilroy-Silk, *Hard Labour* (London: Chatto & Windus, 1988).
5.   P. Seyd, *The Rise and Fall of the Labour Left* (London: Macmillan, 1987) pp. 146–7.
6.   Quoted in D. Wilson, *Battle for Power* (London: Sphere, 1987) p. 302.
7.   D. Owen, *A Future That Will Work* (Harmondsworth: Penguin, 1984) p. 12.
8.   P. Jenkins, *Mrs Thatcher's Revolution: the ending of the socialist era* (London: Jonathan Cape, 1987) p. 243.
9.   P. Seyd, *The Rise and Fall of the Labour Left*, pp. 146–7.
10.   Interview, N. Ridley.
11.   See, for example, A. Henney, *Inside Local Government* (London: Sinclaire Brown, 1984), and L. Chapman, *Waste Away* (London: Chatto & Windus, 1982).
12.   Conservative Manifesto 1987, p. 62.
13.   Interview, Lord Jenkin.
14.   *The Times* (29 June 1983).
15.   M. Leapman, *Kinnock* (London: Unwin Hyman, 1987) p. 103.
16.   Interview, Lord Jenkin.
17.   *The Times* (9 April 1984).
18.   *The Times* (21 January 1986).
19.   Interview, M. Brown.
20.   Interview, Sir B. Braine.
21.   *The Times* (20 January 1986).

CHAPTER 8

1.   P. Riddell, *The Thatcher Government* (London: Martin Robertson, 1983) p. 17.
2.   J. Vincent, *The Times* (10 October 1987).

3. A. Seldon, *The Riddle of the Voucher* (London: IEA, 1986).
4. Seldon, *The Riddle of the Voucher*, p. 89.
5. H. S. Ferns, *How Much Freedom for Universities?* (London: IEA, 1982) p. 36.
6. *London Evening Standard* (30 September 1987).
7. E. Kedourie, *Diamonds into Glass: Government and the Universities* (London: CPS 1988).
8. Roy Strong *Independent*, (8 January 1988).
9. See E. G. West, 'Arts Vouchers to Replace Grants', *Economic Affairs*, 6 (3) (1986).
10. *Daily Telegraph* (3 February 1984).
11. *The Times* (13 February 1984).
12. *Sunday Times* (5 October 1986).
13. *Sunday Times* (28 July 1987).
14. M. Leapman, *The Last Days of the Beeb* (Allen & Unwin, 1986), p. 256.
15. Conservative Party dossier on alleged BBC bias (30 October 1986).
16. *The Times* (3 November 1986).
17. G. Hodgson, *Cut! The BBC and The Politicians* (London: Macmillan, 1988).
18. Interview, L. Brittan.
19. NOP Market Research poll (November 1984).
20. Interview, L. Brittan.
21. M. Leapman, *The Last Days of the Beeb*, p. 125.
22. *The Times* (29 November 1985).

CHAPTER 9

1. Interview, P. Lilley.
2. Interview, Backbench MP.
3. Interview, Cabinet minister.
4. David Butler, *The Times* (27 March 1986).
5. Interview, A. Burt.
6. Interview, junior minister.
7. Interview, Conservative Party official.
8. Interview, G. Gardiner.
9. See R. Tyler *Campaign: the selling of the Prime Minister* (London: Grafton Books, 1987).
10. Interview, Central Office official.
11. Interview, Conservative Whip.
12. Interview, Cabinet minister.
13. Interview, former Cabinet minister.
14. Interview, G. Gardiner.
15. Interview, P. Lilley.
16. S. Ingle, *The British Party System* (Oxford: Basil Blackwell, 1987) p. 220.

17. D. E. Butler and R. Waller, in *The Times Guide to the House of Commons 1987*, p. 256.
18. A. Heath *et al.*, *How Britain Votes* (Oxford: Pergamon, 1985) p. 47.
19. I. Crewe, *Political Studies*, 34 (4) (December 1986) pp. 639–46.
20. D. Denver, review of A. Heath *et al.*, *Political Studies*, 34 (3) (September 1986) p. 485.
21. D. E. Butler and R. Waller, *The Times Guide*, p. 256.
22. Interview, G. Younger.

CHAPTER 10

1. See P. Hennessey and M. Cockerell, *Sources Close to the Prime Minister* (London: Macmillan, 1984) for a useful critical discussion of Mrs Thatcher's relationship with the press.
2. P. Hennessey, *Cabinet* (Oxford: Basil Blackwell, 1986) pp. 102–3.
3. See C. Ponting, *Whitehall: tragedy and farce* (London: Hamish Hamilton, 1986) pp. 216–24.
4. P. Jenkins, *Mrs Thatcher's Revolution: the ending of the socialist era* (London: Jonathan Cape, 1987) p. 185.
5. Interview, Lord Jenkin.
6. Interview, Cabinet minister.
7. Interview, Cabinet minister.
8. Interview, senior Cabinet minister.
9. Interview, Cabinet minister.
10. D. E. Butler and R. Waller, *The Times Guide to the House of Commons 1987*, p. 256.
11. Interview, Conservative Whip.

SELECT BIBLIOGRAPHY

J. E. Alt, *The Politics of Economic Decline* (Oxford: OUP, 1979).

J. Barnett, *Inside the Treasury* (London: André Deutsch, 1982).

P. Bassett, *Strike Free: new industrial relations in Britain* (London: Macmillan, 1987).

J. Bayliss (ed.), *Alternative Approaches to British Defence Policy* (London: Macmillan, 1983).

D. S. Bell (ed.), *The Conservative Government 1979–84* (London: Croom Helm, 1985).

R. Body, *Agriculture: the triumph and the shame* (London: Temple Smith, 1982).

R. Body, *Farming in the Clouds* (London: Temple Smith, 1984).

S. Brittan, *Monetarism and Macro Economics* (London: IEA, 1987).

P. Browning, *The Treasury and Economic Policy, 1964–85* (London: Longman, 1986).

D. E. Butler and R. Waller, *The Times Guide to the House of Commons 1987*.

L. Chapman, *Waste Away* (London: Chatto & Windus, 1982).

F. Chapple, *Sparks Fly* (London: Michael Joseph, 1984).

P. Cockle (ed.), *Public Expenditure Policy 1984–5* (London: Macmillan, 1984).

J. Cole, *The Thatcher Years, a decade of revolution in British politics* (London: BBC, 1987).

R. Cottrell, *The Sacred Cow: the folly of Europe's food mountains* (London: Grafton, 1987).

I. Crewe, *Political Studies* 34 (4) (December 1986).

M. Crick, *Scargill and the Miners* (Harmondsworth: Penguin, 1985).

J. Critchley, *Heseltine* (London: André Deutsch, 1987).

T. Dalyell, *Thatcher: Pattern of Deceit* (London: Cecil Woolf, 1987).

M. Edwardes, *Back From the Brink* (London: Pan, 1983).

H. S. Ferns, *How Much Freedom for Universities?* (London: IEA, 1982).

N. Hagger, *Scargill the Stalinist?* (London: Oak Tree Books, 1984).

P. Hain, *Political Strikes* (Harmondsworth: Penguin Books, 1986).

A. Heath *et al.*, *How Britain Votes* (Oxford: Pergamon, 1985).

P. Hennessey, *Cabinet* (Oxford: Basil Blackwell, 1986).

P. Hennessey and M. Cockerell, *Sources Close the the Prime Minister* (London: Macmillan, 1984).

A. Henney, *Inside Local Government* (London: Sinclair Brown, 1984).

M. Heseltine, *Where There's a Will* (London: Hutchinson, 1987).

B. Hindess, *The Decline of Working Class Politics* (London: MacGibbon & Kee, 1971).

G. Hodgson, *Cut! The BBC and the Politicians* (London: Macmillan, 1988).

M. Holmes, *Political Pressure and Economic Policy: British Government, 1970–4*, (London: Butterworth, 1982).

M. Holmes, *The Labour Government, 1974–9: political aims and economic reality* (London: Macmillan, 1985).

M. Holmes, *The First Thatcher Government, 1979–83: contemporary conservatism and economic change* (Brighton: Wheatsheaf, 1985).

M. Holmes *et al.*, *British Security Policy and the Atlantic Alliance: prospects for the 1990's* (Oxford, Pergamon, 1987).

R. Howarth, *Farming for Farmers?* (London: IEA, 1985).

S. Ingle, *The British Party System* (Oxford: Basil Blackwell, 1987).

M. Jacques, (ed.), *The Politics of Thatcherism* (Edinburgh: Lawrence & Wishart, 1983).

P. Jenkins, *Mrs Thatcher's Revolution: the ending of the socialist era* (London: Jonathan Cape, 1987).

D. Kavanagh, *Thatcherism and British politics: The end of Consensus?* (Oxford: OUP 1987).

J. Kay *et al.*, *Privatisation and Regulation – the UK experience* (Oxford: OUP 1986).

E. Kedourie, *Diamonds into Glass: Government and the Universities* (London: CPS, 1988).

R. Kilroy-Silk, *Hard Labour* (London: Chatto & Windus, 1987).

M. Leapman, *Kinnock* (London: Unwin Hyman 1987).

M. Leapman, *The Last Days of the Beeb* (Allen & Unwin, 1986).

R. Lewis, *Margaret Thatcher* (London: RKP, 1983 edn).

Sir D. MacDougall, *Don and Mandarin* (London: John Murray, 1987).

I. Macgregor, *The Enemies Within* (London: Collins, 1986).

J. MacInnes, *Thatcherism at Work* (London: Open University Press, 1987).

K. Minogue and M. Biddiss, *Thatcherism: personality and politics* (London: Macmillan, 1987).

D. Owen, *A Future That Will Work* (Harmondsworth: Penguin, 1984).

C. Ponting, *Whitehall: tragedy and farce* (London: Hamish Hamilton, 1986).

J. E. Powell, *The Common Market: the case against* (London: Elliott, 1971).

J. Prior, *A Balance of Power* (London: Hamish Hamilton, 1986).

F. Pym, *The Politics of Consent* (London: Sphere, 1985).

P. Riddell, *The Thatcher Government* (London: Martin Robertson, 1983).

A. Roth, *Heath and the Heathmen* (London: RKP, 1972).

A. Seldon, *The Riddle of the Voucher* (London: IEA, 1986).

P. Seyd, *The Rise and Fall of the Labour Left* (London: Macmillan, 1987).

G. Thompson, *The Conservatives' Economic Policy* (London: Croom Helm, 1986).

R. Tyler, *Campaign: the selling of the Prime Minister* (London: Grafton Books, 1987).

C. Veljanovski, *Selling the State* (London: Weidenfeld & Nicolson, 1987).

C. Veljanovski, *Economic Affairs*, 7 (3) (1987).

John Vincent, 'Margaret Thatcher: her place in history', *Contemporary Record* 1 (3) (1987).

A. Walters, *Britain's Economic Renaissance* (Oxford: OUP, 1986).

N. Wapshott and G. Brock, *Thatcher* (London: Futura, 1983).

E. G. West, 'Arts Vouchers to Replace Grants', *Economic Affairs*, (March 1986).

D. Wilson, *Battle for Power* (London: Sphere, 1987).

INDEX

169